Google Nexus 7 Tablet

CHRIS FEHILY

D1275813

 Peachpit Press

Visual QuickStart Guide
Google Nexus 7 Tablet
Chris Fehily

Peachpit Press
1249 Eighth Street
Berkeley, CA 94710
510/524-2178
510/524-2221 (fax)

Find us on the Web at www.peachpit.com.
To report errors, please send a note to errata@peachpit.com.
Peachpit Press is a division of Pearson Education.

Executive editor: Clifford Colby
Editor: Kathy Simpson
Production editor: Becky Winter
Compositor: Danielle Foster
Indexer: Valerie Haines Perry
Cover design: RHDG / Riezebos Holzbaur Design Group, Peachpit Press
Interior design: Peachpit Press
Logo design: MINE™ www.minesf.com

ISBN-13: 978-0-321-88734-4
ISBN-10: 0-321-88734-4

9 8 7 6 5 4 3 2 1

Printed and bound in the United States of America

Table of Contents

1

Getting Started

To use a Nexus 7 tablet, you need to know a few basics. This chapter brings you up to speed with a few terms and concepts, and shows you how to set up a new, out-of-the-box Nexus 7.

In This Chapter

Touring the Hardware and Specifications

Ⓐ and Ⓑ label the Nexus 7's physical controls and ports, which are covered in detail later in this chapter and beyond. You can refer to these figures to jog your memory.

TIP The 4-pin connector is used with Nexus 7 dock accessories, which cradle the Nexus for charging, hands-free viewing, and line-out audio.

Table 1.1 lists some key specifications for the Nexus 7. For a complete list, see www.google.com/nexus/#/7/specs.

The Nexus 7 comes with several accessories:

- A *USB charging unit,* used to provide power and charge the battery. This unit varies by country or region. Don't use a different unit to charge your Nexus 7.

- A *Micro-USB cable,* used to connect your Nexus 7 to the USB charging unit or to your computer.

TABLE 1.1 Nexus 7 Specifications

Specification	Nexus 7
Dimensions	7.81" × 4.72" × 0.41" (198.5mm × 120mm × 10.45mm)
Weight	0.75 pounds (340 grams)
Display size	7" (177.8mm) diagonal
Display resolution	1280 × 800 pixels (216 pixels per inch)
Processors	Quad-core Tegra 3 processor
Memory (RAM)	1 GB
Storage	8 GB or 16 GB flash memory
Wireless	Wi-Fi 802.11 b/g/n Bluetooth
Battery life	9–10 hours
Camera	1.2 megapixels (front-facing)

TIP To see the guts of a dismantled Nexus 7, go to www.ifixit.com, search for *nexus 7,* and then click the Nexus 7 Teardown link.

Nexus 7 vs. iPad

Though it lacks a few of the Apple iPad's high-end features, the Nexus 7 is designed to do its main jobs as an inexpensive Internet terminal and media player extremely well. It's easy to configure and easy to use, offers fluid video and animation, and is solidly built, not giving you any sense that Google skimped to keep the price down.

By contrast with the iPad, the Nexus 7 has no 3G/4G modem (for connecting to cellular networks) and no rear-facing camera, and it has a lower-resolution display—216 ppi (pixels per inch) vs. the iPad's 264 ppi. In the plus column, the Nexus doesn't lock you into Apple's closed ecosystem; Google's garden grows a bit wilder. Also, the Nexus's replaceable battery and clip-fastened (rather than glued) case means that any PC shop can fix it—unlike the iPad, which is hard and expensive to repair. For voice search and commands, Nexus's Google Now and Google Search (Chapters 9 and 10) compare favorably with Apple's Siri. Finally, Google's mapping and navigation features are vastly superior to Apple's versions. You can shop for apps, media, and books in the Google Play store (Chapter 16), which is similar to Apple's App Store, iTunes Store, and iBookstore.

Personally, I'm conflicted about the Nexus relative to the iPad, so for now, I carry both devices. Sigh.

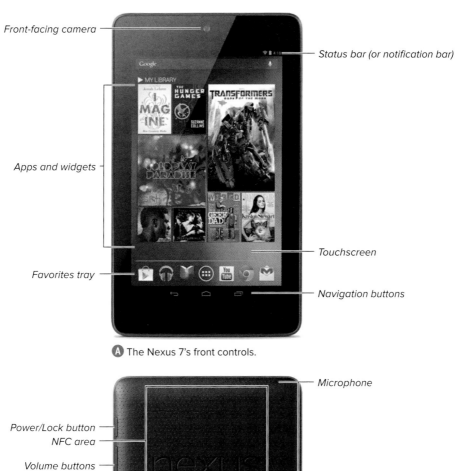

Front-facing camera

Status bar (or notification bar)

Apps and widgets

Touchscreen

Favorites tray

Navigation buttons

A The Nexus 7's front controls.

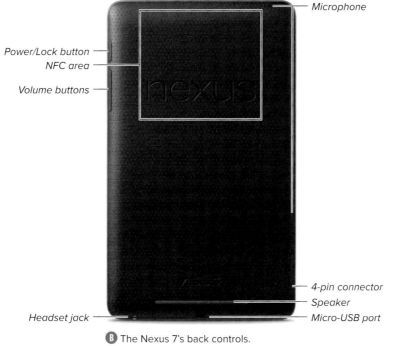

Microphone

Power/Lock button

NFC area

Volume buttons

4-pin connector

Speaker

Headset jack

Micro-USB port

B The Nexus 7's back controls.

Using and Updating Android

The Nexus 7's operating system, called *Android,* is the same OS that runs on many other (non-Apple, non-Microsoft) tablets and smartphones . Android adapts to the hardware and screen on which it's running but retains its basic personality across all devices, so if you've used an Android smartphone (such as those from Samsung, LG, HTC, or Motorola), you have a head start with the Nexus 7.

Android was developed by the Open Handset Alliance (OHA), a group of firms that develops and advances open standards and is led by Google. By *led,* I mean that it's really the iron fist of Google that steers and develops Android; all the rest are hangers-on.

Android is based on Linux (a flavor of the industrial-strength Unix operating system) and is *open-source,* meaning that it's developed in a public manner, and others can study, change, improve, and at times distribute it.

Android has a large number of software developers writing apps that you can download from the Google Play store (formerly called Android Market), covered in Chapter 16.

TIP To view or change advanced Android options, tap Settings > Developer Options. Many of these settings are designed for professional developers, so be careful.

Ⓐ The Android Robot logo means that a device runs Android.

Shorthand Instructions

Throughout this book, you'll find shorthand instructions like "Tap Settings > Wi-Fi > On," which means this: On the Home screen or All Apps screen, tap the Settings app and then slide Wi-Fi to On. (To see the Settings icon, you may have to tap the All Apps icon ⊞ in the Favorites tray.) Each name between the > symbols refers to an app, widget, icon, button, link, or control; just look on the screen for a matching label.

B The About Tablet screen gives hardware, software, and status information about your Nexus and Android.

Google regularly releases free updates and bug fixes for Android. Some changes refine or add features to Android and the built-in apps, whereas others plug security holes or fix stability problems. Your Nexus will notify you automatically when an update is available, but you can check manually at any time. You can update to the latest version of Android over Wi-Fi. Before you update your Nexus, plug it in or make sure that it has a significant battery charge.

TIP To change the size of the text used throughout Android, tap **Settings** > **Display** > **Font Size**. If you have vision, hearing, or mobility problems, tap **Settings** > **Accessibility** to make Android easier to use.

To get system information:

Tap Settings > About Tablet **B**.

To update Android:

1. Tap Settings > About Tablet > System Updates Ⓑ.

2. If an update is available, tap Restart & Install Ⓒ.

TIP **Android versions (and significant incremental updates) are named after desserts or sweets. This books covers Android 4.1, better known as Jelly Bean.**

Ⓒ The System Updates screen tells you whether an updated version of Android is available and, if so, describes its changes.

Pure Android

Because the Nexus 7 is a Google-branded product, its Android software is "pure," meaning that it's exactly how Google designed it, with no extra changes or add-ons.

Google gives away Android, however, and any company can use the OS on its smartphones, tablets, and other hardware. To differentiate their products, manufacturers modify standard Android by adding custom Home screens, controls, apps, widgets, and other doodads. These "enhancements" are often user-hostile, self-promoting, or poorly designed. My Samsung Galaxy Tab tablet, for example, is stuffed with Samsung-only apps that let me chat with *only* Galaxy Tab users, share photos with *only* other Samsung owners, and so on. What's more, this crapware occupies about 25 percent of already-tight storage and can't be deleted without *rooting* the machine (a tricky technical procedure on Samsung hardware).

Pure Android offers advantages besides peace of mind. You can always update your Nexus to the latest version of Android, whereas updating non-Google devices is often an adventure. And virtually every app that you buy from the Google Play store will work on pure Android, which isn't true of the many fragmented, nonpure versions.

Rooting a pure Android device is easy, should you want to experiment, install custom or rogue apps, and do other things that you can't do on an iPad. Pure Android is one of the Nexus 7's best features, but Google doesn't trumpet it so as not to step on the toes of the other hardware vendors.

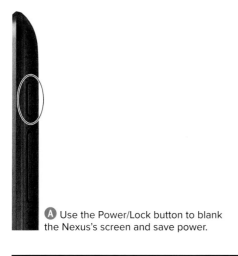

(A) Use the Power/Lock button to blank the Nexus's screen and save power.

Powering On and Off

Putting a Nexus 7 to *sleep* locks it in standby mode: The screen turns off and doesn't respond to taps, but audio keeps playing, and the volume buttons still work. The battery drains slowly but noticeably. A sleeping Nexus *wakes* instantly to where you last left off. You may also need to wake your Nexus if you leave it untended for a few minutes, because it goes to sleep by itself to save power.

Powering off a Nexus shuts it down: No power is used, though the battery still drains imperceptibly over days or weeks. A powered-off Nexus takes a minute to *power on* and show the Lock screen.

> **TIP** In day-to-day use, you don't need to power off; sleep suffices in most cases.

To put your Nexus 7 to sleep:

Press the Power/Lock button (A).

To wake your Nexus 7:

Press the Power/Lock button and then unlock the screen (B).

The first time that you use a new Nexus 7, you unlock it by dragging the lock icon out of the circle. For details, see "Setting the Screen Lock" in Chapter 3.

> **TIP** To adjust how long your Nexus screen stays on before it sleeps (and displays the Lock screen when you wake it), tap **Settings > Display > Sleep.**

12:30

Mon, August 13

(B) The Nexus locks itself because, as with any touchscreen device, an unintended tap on the screen while it's in your bag or backpack can launch a program and drain the battery.

To power off your Nexus 7:

1. Press and hold the Power/Lock button for a moment until a dialog box appears.

2. Tap Power Off.

To power on your Nexus 7:

Press the Power/Lock button.

TIP To set a secure screen lock that you must enter each time that you wake or power on your Nexus 7, see "Setting the Screen Lock" in Chapter 3.

Restarting: A Quick Fix

The Nexus 7 does a good job of fixing its own problems, but it can accumulate software baggage with time and use. *Restarting* your Nexus (powering it off and then back on again) can quickly solve many common problems, including unexpected app failure, short battery life, odd hardware behavior, slow app or Android response, and sync issues. A restart does all the following:

- Safely quits all active applications, and processes and closes all open files, preserving your data

- Frees CPU and memory (RAM) resources

- Powers off all hardware components

For other troubleshooting tips, see "Managing Apps and Services" and "Optimizing Data Usage" in Chapter 2.

Using Multitouch Gestures

The Nexus 7 is designed for your finger-tips. You interact with the software on the screen by performing the *multitouch gestures,* or simply *gestures,* described in **Table 1.2**. If you've used a computer mouse, learning these gestures will be easy because tapping and dragging correspond to similar mouse actions. Unfamiliar motions like swiping and pinching quickly become natural.

> **TIP** To hear a sound when you tap the screen, tap Settings > **Sound** > **Touch Sounds.**

TABLE 1.2 Multitouch Gestures

To	Do This
Tap (or touch)	Gently tap the screen with one finger. A tap triggers the default action for a given item.
Double-tap	Tap twice quickly. (If you tap too slowly, your Nexus interprets it as two single taps.) A double tap is a quick way to zoom in on a photo or Web page.
Touch and hold (or long-press)	Touch the screen with your finger, and maintain contact with the glass (typically, until some onscreen action happens).
Drag	Touch and hold a point on the screen and then slide your finger across the glass to a different part of the screen.
Swipe (or flick or slide)	Fluidly and decisively whip your finger across the screen. If you're on a Web page or a list, a faster swipe scrolls the screen faster.
Pinch	Touch your thumb and index finger to the screen; then pinch those digits together (to zoom out) or spread them apart (to zoom in).
Rotate	Spread your thumb and index finger and touch them to the screen; then rotate those digits clockwise or counterclockwise. (Or keep your fingers steady and rotate the Nexus itself.)

The Nexus 7's *capacitive* screen contains a dense grid of touch sensors that responds to the electrical field of your fingers. The screen won't respond to a traditional stylus (and you can't wear gloves). Increasing finger pressure on a capacitive screen, as opposed to a resistive screen, won't increase responsiveness.

TIP The frame surrounding the screen is called the *bezel*. The bezel doesn't respond to gestures; it's just a place to rest your thumbs.

Feel free to use two hands. You can use both hands to type on the Nexus's onscreen keyboard, for example. In some apps, you can touch and hold an item with a finger of one hand and then use your other hand to tap other items to select them all as a group. If you're having trouble with a gesture, make sure that you're not touching the screen's edge with a stray thumb or finger (of either hand).

TIP Some apps, such as People, use index lists (A, B, C...) along an edge to help you navigate quickly. To scroll though an a index, drag your finger along it, or tap a letter to jump to items starting with that letter. Tap an item to open it.

Using a Mouse

You can connect a mouse (or trackpad) to your Nexus via USB or Bluetooth and then use it just as you would with a computer. For USB connections, you may need an adapter to connect the mouse to the Nexus's Micro-USB port. To connect a Bluetooth mouse, see "Bluetooth Devices" in Chapter 5. Bluetooth and unpowered USB connections drain the battery quickly. To connect multiple USB devices, use a powered USB hub.

When you connect a mouse to your Nexus, a pointer appears, just like on a computer. Use it as follows:

- Moving the mouse moves the pointer. To adjust the pointer speed, tap Settings > Language & Input > Pointer Speed.

- Clicking, holding down, or dragging with the mouse button is equivalent to tapping, touching and holding, or dragging with your finger. (Only one mouse button is supported.)

- The mouse trackball or scroll wheel (if present) scrolls vertically or horizontally.

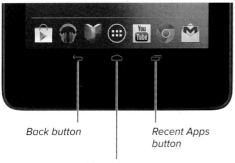

Back button

Recent Apps button

Home button

Ⓐ The navigation buttons.

Ⓑ On a new Nexus 7, the central Home screen looks similar to this.

Using the Navigation Buttons

No matter what you're doing on your Nexus 7, you'll find three *navigation buttons* at the bottom of the screen **Ⓐ**. In some apps, these buttons shrink to dots or disappear with disuse. To bring them back, tap their location.

- **⬅ Back button.** Opens the last screen that you were working in, even if it was in a different app. If you back up to the Home screen, you can't go back any further.

- **⌂ Home button.** Opens the Home screen. If you're viewing a left or right Home screen, it jumps to the central Home screen **Ⓑ**. For details, see "Navigating and Organizing the Home Screen" in Chapter 2.

continues on next page

- 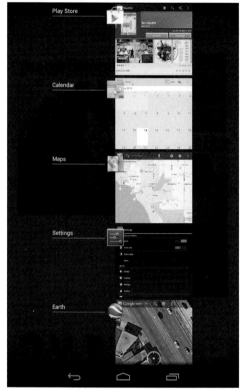 **Recent Apps button.** Opens a list of apps that you've used recently **C**. To scroll the list, swipe it. To open an app, tap its thumbnail. To remove an app from the list, swipe its thumbnail left or right. To see the app's menu, touch and hold its thumbnail.

TIP **When you're typing on the onscreen keyboard, the Back button changes to the modified Back button ⌄, which you can tap to hide the keyboard.**

Because the Nexus 7 displays only one app at a time, you can use the navigation buttons to switch among apps. If you're browsing the Web in Chrome, for example, when your Nexus chimes an incoming-email alert, tap a navigation button to close Chrome and then open Gmail, where you can read your mail. If the desired app isn't visible, tap ⌂ and then tap ⊞ in the Favorites tray (above the navigation buttons) to view all your apps.

Tapping a navigation button always saves your current position or work in progress automatically. (Unlike Windows and OS X programs, Android apps have no manual Save command.) If you're watching a video in Play Movies & TV or typing a message in Gmail and then tap Home, you can return to Play Movies & TV or Gmail at any time, exactly as you left off.

C Each thumbnail image in the list shows the app in the state in which you last left it.

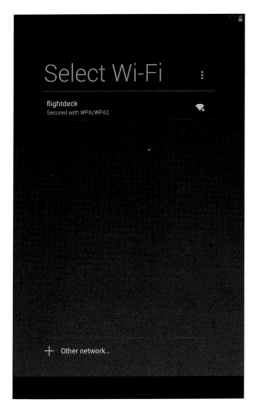

A Setup lists in-range Wi-Fi networks. A secured home network is safer than a public network at a café or library, where miscreant geeks can sniff out your passwords and personal information as you type.

Selling Your Old Nexus 7

Before you sell or give away a Nexus 7, reset it to erase all your personal data, accounts, and settings so that the new owner can't access your stuff. Resetting a Nexus 7 returns it to its factory settings without reinstalling Android. Tap Settings > Backup & Reset > Factory Data Reset > Reset Tablet. Charge the battery before a reset.

Setting Up Your Nexus 7

The first thing to do with a new, out-of-the-box Nexus 7 is set it up. To do so, you need a nearby wireless Internet connection. (Don't wander away from the Wi-Fi signal with your Nexus during setup.) Your Nexus will also need a significant battery charge if the battery drained while sitting in the cargo container or on the store shelf; see "Charging the Battery" in Chapter 2.

TIP The Nexus 7 is self-contained. You don't need a computer to set up or use it. Everything that you need is downloaded over the Internet. Your account data and settings are backed up wirelessly to the cloud (free online storage).

To set up your new Nexus 7, turn it on and then follow the onscreen instructions, which step you through the setup process. Along the way, you're asked to

- Choose your preferred language (possibly including country or region) for the Nexus 7's screens, keyboard, and interface.

- Connect to a Wi-Fi network **A**. A 🔒 icon indicates a secure network (which requires a password), and 📶 indicates the signal strength (more bars = stronger signal). For details, see "Wi-Fi Connections" in Chapter 5.

TIP To join a closed network—one whose name is hidden so that it isn't shown in the list of scanned networks—tap Other Network.

continues on next page

- Sign in with or create a Google Account . Your Google Account is a unique user ID (email address) and password that lets you use the Google Play store, back up and sync your data, and use other Google apps and services. See the "Google Accounts" sidebar for details.

TIP **If you bought your Nexus 7 directly from the Google Play store, Setup enters your Gmail address automatically.**

- Join Google+, Google's social network (basically, Google's version of Facebook). You can skip this step if you're not interested. For information about Google+, go to https://plus.google.com.

- Enter credit-card info to shop in the Google Play store for apps, books, music, movies, and other media. If you like, you can skip this step and set up your store account later in the Play Store app.

B To sign in to your Google Account, enter the email address that you use for Gmail, YouTube, Google Apps, AdWords, or any other Google product. If you have multiple Google Accounts, you can add the others later by tapping Settings > Add Account (see Chapter 6).

Google Accounts

A Google Account lets you organize and access your personal information from your Nexus 7 or any computer or mobile device, as follows:

- **Google Play store:** You can shop for and download movies, TV shows, books, music, magazines, apps, and more. Your Google Account lets you reach any of your content from any of your devices.

- **Google Wallet:** You can connect your Google Account with Google Wallet to pay for purchases in Google Play and other online stores. Google Wallet is a secure mobile payment system (similar to PayPal) that lets you store debit cards, credit cards, loyalty cards, gift cards, and more.

- **Back up and sync:** Google securely and continually backs up your email, text messages, calendar events, contacts, and more, and it syncs your data across computers and devices on which you use the same Google Account. You can access your stuff no matter what computer or device you're using.

- **Google apps and services:** Your Google Account gives you personalized access to Google apps and services, including Gmail, Google Maps, Navigation, Google Play, YouTube, Google Talk, and Messaging.

- Set backup and restore options for your apps, settings, and other data **C**. If you previously backed up your Google Account, you can restore it here (see "Backing Up or Erasing Your Data" in Chapter 6).
- Set Location Services options **D**. For details, see "Location Services" in Chapter 17.

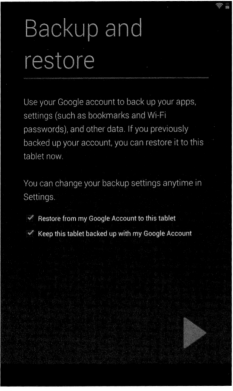

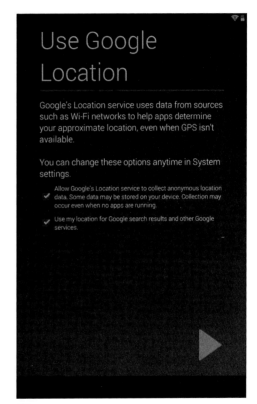

C If you choose to restore your Google Account to your Nexus 7, your Home screen, apps, settings, and other data will be downloaded to your tablet.

D Location Services lets built-in apps such as Maps and Google Search, as well as third-party apps such as weather apps, use your physical whereabouts via the Nexus 7's built-in positioning service. This service is a convenience for some people and a privacy invasion for others.

When you're done, tap  to go to the Home screen Ⓔ. Your Nexus 7 is set up and ready to use.

TIP If you change your mind or skip a step during setup, you can change the setup options later by using the Settings app. To change the system language, tap **Settings > Language**. To sign in to, change, or create a Google Account, tap **Settings > Accounts**. To toggle Location Services, tap **Settings > Location Services**. To change backup settings, tap **Settings > Backup & Reset**.

Ⓔ The Home screen's exact appearance depends on whether you set up your device as a new Nexus 7 or restored it from a Google Account backup.

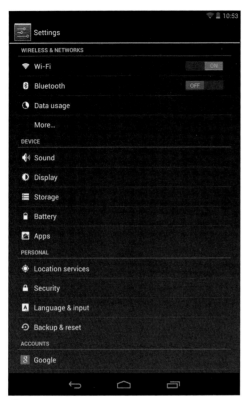

A The Settings screen.

Viewing and Changing Settings

Settings is the central screen for changing systemwide settings and getting information about your Nexus 7, similar to Preferences on the Mac or Control Panel in Windows. If you've used your Nexus 7 for even a little while, you've probably visited Settings.

If you want to tweak the way your Nexus 7 works, poke around in Settings to see what's available.

To view or change settings:

1. Tap the Settings icon on the Home screen.

   If the Settings app isn't visible, tap ⌂ and then tap ⊞ in the Favorites tray (above the navigation buttons) to view all your apps.

   or

   Swipe down from the top of the screen and then tap the small Settings icon ⊟ at the top of the notification shade.

   The Settings screen opens A.

   TIP **To change the text size in Settings (and elsewhere throughout Android), tap Settings > Display > Font Size.**

continues on next page

2. Tap an item to view or change a setting .

If necessary, swipe up or down to scroll the list to the desired setting.

3. To backtrack to the previous screen, tap the Settings icon in the top-left corner of the screen.

TIP To change the settings for a specific app, open the app and then tap its menu icon at the top or bottom of the screen.

B These settings show options for changing the display. Tapping an item may take you to yet another Settings screen or launch a dialog box where you can view or change the current settings.

2

Touring Your Nexus 7

Google's Nexus 7 offers the features of modern tablets: You can surf the Web; play games; find your way with maps; download and play media; keep in touch via email, messaging, or video chat; and much more (including a few Google-specific touches). Yet behind its fair face, the Nexus 7 is a true computer running complex programs on a modern operating system. Fortunately, Google has given the Nexus a consistent, simple design that lets you wield a lot of power with only a little learning. Even complete beginners can't easily stumble into any ravines. This chapter gets you up and running.

In This Chapter

Navigating and Organizing the Home Screen

After you unlock your Nexus 7, the *Home screen* appears, displaying icons for your apps and widgets **A**. The Nexus 7 comes with built-in apps and widgets (Gmail, Settings, and My Library, for example), and you can download more from the Google Play store, Google's online store for media and Android apps (see Chapter 16). You can customize the layout of apps icons and widgets on the Home screen and in the Favorites tray.

TIP The Home screen can't rotate to landscape (wide) view out of the box, but the third-party app Ultimate Rotation Control (available in the Google Play store) can override rotation defaults.

Widgets

Apps

Home screen

Favorites tray

Navigation buttons

A The Home screen.

Tap to open the Google Play store to learn more.

Tap to suppress future suggestions like this one.

Tap to see a new suggestion.

B The Recommended Apps widget suggests featured apps, popular apps, and apps based on the ones that you already have installed.

Open a folder of popular apps.

Shop in the Google Play store.

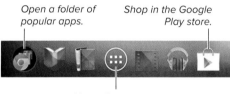

View all your apps and widgets.

C The Favorites tray.

Apps. *Apps* (short for *applications*) are conventional programs that occupy the entire screen when opened. Applications added to the Home screen appear as icons. To open an app, tap its icon.

Widgets. *Widgets* are single-purpose miniprograms. Widgets added to the Home screen appear as icons that you can tap to open or as tiles that you can resize to occupy part or all of the Home screen. Every widget is different, so you may have to experiment with its links and controls to figure out how it works **B**. When you set up a new Nexus 7, the Home screen shows the My Library widget (visible in **A**), which displays your most recently used music, books, and so on, as well as freebies and promotions from Google.

TIP For PC or Mac users: Android widgets are similar to Windows gadgets or OS X dashboard widgets.

Home screen. If you install lots of apps and widgets, you can spread them over the multiple Home screens that reside to the left or right of the central Home screen. The central Home screen appears by default.

Favorites tray. You can put your most frequently used apps in the Favorites tray, which is visible at the bottom of every Home screen **C**. Anchored to the center of the tray is the All Apps icon, which shows all your apps and widgets.

Navigation buttons. The three navigation buttons at the bottom of the screen take you to the previous screen, the Home screen, or the Recent Apps screen. For details, see "Using the Navigation Buttons" in Chapter 1.

To show the Home screen:

Tap the Home button ⌂.

TIP The navigation buttons are always available at the bottom of the screen. If they shrink to dots or fade away, tap their location to bring them back.

To switch Home screens:

Swipe left or right on the Home screen.

As you switch screens, the thin bar above the Favorites tray glows to show which Home screen you're on.

TIP If you're on any Home screen, tapping ⌂ switches to the central Home screen.

To rearrange Home-screen icons:

Touch and hold an app or widget icon for a moment and then drag it slowly to a new location within a screen or off the edge of one screen and onto the next.

As you drag, other icons move aside (if there's room).

TIP If you drop an app icon on top of another app icon, you create a folder, covered in "Creating Home-Screen Folders" later in this chapter.

To resize a widget:

1. On the Home screen, touch and hold the widget for a moment until it rises slightly out of the screen; then lift your finger.

   A blue border appears on the widget.

2. Drag any of the dots on the widget's border **D**.

   As you drag, other apps and widgets move aside (if there's room).

3. When you're done resizing, tap an empty area of the Home screen.

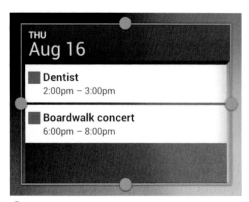

D Drag the blue dots to resize the widget.

Switching Apps

The Nexus 7 displays only one app at a time, full-screen. You can't have, say, Chrome on one side of the screen and Gmail on the other, as you can in Windows or OS X. Fortunately, Android supports *multitasking,* which lets multiple apps run in the background at the same time, and you can quickly open, switch among, and close apps.

Most apps are effectively frozen when you switch away from them, but certain apps (such as Play Music and Gmail) continue working in the background. Switching back to an app lets you resume where you left off. To switch apps, use the navigation buttons at the bottom of the screen.

See also "Managing Apps and Services" later in this chapter.

E The Nexus 7 comes with a built-in collection of apps...

F ...and widgets.

To add apps or widgets to the Home screen:

1. If necessary, tap ⌂ to go to the Home screen.

2. Tap ⊞ in the Favorites tray.

   The All Apps screen opens, showing your installed apps **E** and widgets **F**.

3. Swipe left or right to find the desired app or widget.

   You can also tap Apps or Widgets in the top-left corner to jump to a specific section.

4. Touch and hold the app or widget icon.

   The display jumps to the Home screen.

5. Drag the icon to the desired Home screen location and then lift your finger.

   You can drag off the edge of one screen and onto the next.

> **TIP** You can't drag an icon to a Home screen that lacks the room to hold it.

To remove an app or widget from the Home screen:

1. Touch and hold the app or widget icon for a moment until the word *Remove* appears at the top of the screen.

2. Drag the icon to *Remove* and then lift your finger.

   The app or widget is removed from the Home screen (but isn't removed from your Nexus).

Creating Home-Screen Folders

If too many icons are crowding your Home screens, you can group them into *folders* rather than drag them around to different screens. It's a common practice to create multiple folders, each holding similar types of apps (games, media, travel, and so on). Folders save a lot of screen space and reduce excessive screen-switching. Folders can hold apps but not widgets or other (nested) folders.

To create a folder:

1. Touch and hold an app icon for a moment and then drag it on top of an app icon that you want to store in the same folder.

   A new folder containing the two icons is created .

2. If you like, drag other icons to the folder.

3. Do any of the following:

   ▸ To open the folder, tap it **B**.

   ▸ Tap an app icon in the folder to open that app.

   ▸ Drag icons within the folder to rearrange them.

   ▸ Drag icons out of the folder. Removing the last icon from a folder deletes the folder.

   ▸ To rename the folder, open it, tap the default name (*Unnamed Folder*), and then type a new name. The onscreen keyboard appears when you tap the name.

   ▸ To close the folder, tap an empty area of the Home screen or tap the Home button ⌂.

A A folder appears on the Home screen as a black circle containing small icons.

| Earth | Chrome | Gmail |
| Maps | Settings | Gallery |

Unnamed Folder

B An open folder.

TIP By default, the leftmost icon in the Favorites tray (near the bottom of the Home screen) is a folder containing popular Google apps. As with any folder, you can customize its contents.

Viewing the Status Bar

The *status bar* (also called the *notification bar*) is the narrow strip that runs along the top of the Home screen, the Lock screen, and many application screens Ⓐ. The status bar shows the current time and displays icons that indicate the current state of your Nexus, including pending notifications (see Chapter 8), Bluetooth status, Wi-Fi network connectivity and signal strength, and battery level and charging status.

Pending
notifications

Bluetooth, Wi-Fi,
and battery
status   Clock

Ⓐ A glance at the status bar can tell you whether all is well with your Nexus.

Setting the Date and Time

The time of day appears in the status bar at the top of the screen. By default, the time and time zone are set automatically, based on your Internet connection. By tapping Settings > Date & Time to display the Date & Time screen 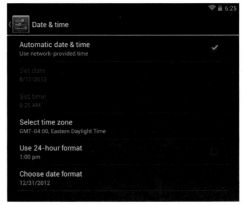, you can switch between the 12-hour (AM/PM) clock and 24-hour clock, and also choose a date format (the order of the year, month, and day). If you're traveling, you can choose a time zone and set your Nexus's date and time manually. Keep your Nexus's time accurate; apps use it to time-stamp files and messages, schedule tasks, record events, and sound alerts.

TIP To display the time, day, and date in large format on the Home screen, open the Clock app. An Analog Clock widget is also available. Both app and widget also let you set alarms.

Ⓐ The Date & Time screen.

 If you're going to read for a long time, a dim screen is less fatiguing than a bright one.

The Ambient Light Sensor

When Automatic Brightness is turned on, the Nexus autoadjusts brightness by using its built-in ambient light sensor. This sensor, located near the front camera, is barely visible behind the screen's bezel. If the screen doesn't dim automatically, check whether something (your hand, a protective film, or a case) is blocking or obscuring the sensor.

Adjusting Screen Brightness

You can make the Nexus's screen brighter or dimmer, or have it adjust the brightness automatically for ambient light.

To adjust screen brightness:

1. Tap Settings > Display > Brightness Ⓐ.

2. To make the Nexus autoadjust brightness for current light conditions, turn on Automatic Brightness.

   or

   To adjust brightness manually, turn off Automatic Brightness and then drag the slider.

Changing the Wallpaper

You can choose the picture or animation that you want to use as a background image, or *wallpaper,* for your Home screen . The Nexus comes with some stock images and animations for use as wallpaper, but you can use your own photo from the Gallery app.

> **TIP** You can download additional wallpapers from the Google Play store. Open the store and then search for *wallpaper* or browse the Live Wallpaper category. For details, see Chapter 16.

To change the wallpaper:

1. Touch and hold an empty area of the Home screen until the Choose Wallpaper From dialog box appears **B**.

2. Tap a wallpaper source:

   ▸ **Gallery.** Choose a picture that you've stored or synced on your Nexus (see Chapter 18).

   ▸ **Live Wallpapers.** Choose an animated wallpaper.

   ▸ **Wallpapers.** Choose a static image from the scrolling list.

3. If you chose Gallery, tap the image, drag or resize the image's crop area, and then tap OK.

   or

   If you chose Live Wallpapers or Wallpapers, tap Set Wallpaper.

> **TIP** You can also change the wallpaper by tapping Settings > Display > Wallpaper.

A Wallpaper sits behind the icons and widgets on your Home screen.

B Choose the type of wallpaper you want.

Changing Screen Orientation

The Nexus's built-in accelerometer senses how you're holding the Nexus in physical space and then orients the screen to either portrait (tall) or landscape (wide) view .

To change the view, rotate the Nexus. Most apps self-adjust to fit the new orientation. Some apps support only one view. Many games and video players, for example, work only in landscape view.

TIP The third-party app Ultimate Rotation Control (available in the Google Play store) can override rotation defaults.

If you don't want the screen to change its orientation, such as when you're reading while lying on your side, you can lock the current view to stop it from rotating. To do so, swipe down from the top of the screen and then tap ⬦ at the top of the notification shade **B**. Tap it again to unlock rotation.

A The same Web page in portrait and landscape views. In Chrome, Web pages scale automatically to the wider screen, making the text and images larger.

Tap to lock or unlock screen rotation.

B You can lock the screen orientation in its current view.

Adjusting the Volume

The buttons on the right edge of the Nexus control the volume 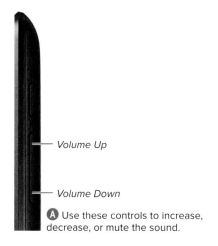. The volume control is a rocker switch with two buttons that adjust the audio level of anything that makes noise, such as songs, videos, audio-books, apps, notifications, and alarms.

Volume adjustments affect the Nexus's built-in speaker, earphones or headsets plugged into the headphone jack, and external speakers connected wirelessly or through the Micro-USB port or 4-pin connector.

To change the volume, press the Volume Up or Volume Down button. To raise or lower the volume quickly, press and hold the button. An audio-level overlay appears briefly onscreen as you adjust the volume **B**.

TIP **To set the volume levels of media, notifications, and alarms independently, tap Settings > Sound > Volumes.**

To quickly mute all sound, press and hold the Power/Lock button for a moment and then tap Silent Mode. Repeat the gesture to toggle sound back on. When sound is muted, appears in the status bar at the top of the screen.

Volume Up

Volume Down

A Use these controls to increase, decrease, or mute the sound.

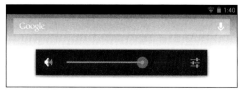

B You can also drag the slider to adjust to change the volume.

 The headset jack.

Using Earphones and Speakers

The Nexus doesn't come with earphones, but it does have a headset jack on its bottom-right edge . More precisely, it has a standard 3.5mm stereo headphone minijack. You can plug in any earphones or headsets that come with the 3.5mm miniplug (including iPod and iPhone earphones). Push the plug firmly into the jack so that it fully connects.

Certain audio accessories, such as stereo-audio docks and external speakers, plug into the Nexus's Micro-USB port or 4-pin connector, or connect wirelessly via Bluetooth. To pair wireless speakers with your Nexus, tap Settings > Bluetooth > On. After the Nexus finds and lists your accessory, tap its name; then, if required, type a passkey (which you'll find in the gadget's manual).

The Nexus's built-in speaker—the slot near the bottom of the rear panel— is silenced when you use earphones or external speakers.

Charging the Battery

Charge your Nexus by using only the USB charging unit and Micro-USB cable that came with it (or that you bought separately from Google). The charging unit varies by country or region, so don't risk using other charging units even if they look compatible, including third-party units like the Apple USB power adapter.

The battery icon in the status bar at the top of the screen shows the battery strength and charging status .

You can also charge your Nexus via a USB port on your computer, provided that the Nexus is sleeping or powered off (see "Powering On and Off" in Chapter 1). Charging through a USB port takes longer than charging with the USB charging unit.

TIP A drained Nexus lacks sufficient power to show the Home screen. You may have to charge it for a few minutes to see the Home screen.

A A lightning bolt indicates that the battery is charging. A red battery icon means the battery is running low. An exclamation point means it's almost drained.

To check the battery level and usage details, tap Settings > Battery . Near the top of the Battery screen are the battery level (as a percentage of full charge), battery status (full, charging, or discharging), and power source if charging (USB or AC). The discharge graph shows battery level over time and how long you've been running on battery power. Below the graph is a list that breaks down battery usage by apps and services. Tap an item in the list for more details .

B The Battery screen shows the current battery status, graphs the discharge history, and lists the power hogs.

C The Use Details screen varies by app or service. Some apps include buttons to let you change settings that affect power usage, or stop the app completely.

Conserving Power

When you're not using your Nexus, put it to sleep (by pressing the Power/Lock button) to conserve power. When you're using it, the battery drains more slowly if you

- Dim the screen brightness (tap Settings > Display > Brightness).

- Turn off Wi-Fi, VPN, and Bluetooth connections when you're not using them (see Chapter 5).

TIP You can switch to airplane mode to turn off all wireless connections in one shot. Press and hold the Power/Lock button for a moment and then tap Airplane Mode, Alternatively, tap Settings > More (below Wireless & Networks) > Airplane Mode.

- Turn off or minimize the use of Location Services (Settings > Location Services).

- Don't leave the Maps or Navigation apps open onscreen when you're not using them. They use GPS (and, thus, more power) only when they're running.

- Shorten sleep timeout (tap Settings > Display > Sleep).

- Sync manually. Turn off automatic syncing for all apps by tapping Settings > Google (below Accounts) > *account_ name*. When automatic syncing is turned off, you won't receive notifications of new messages, new email, and recently updated information.

Cleaning the Screen

The Nexus's glass touchscreen has a special coating that does its best to repel fingerprints, but eventually, it will accumulate oils, glazed sugar, sunscreen, or whatever else you have on your hands. To clean the screen, wipe it gently with a soft, lint-free cloth—the same kind that you use to clean eyeglasses or camera lenses.

To clean the rest of the Nexus, unplug it from any docks or USB cables and then turn it off. (Press and hold the Power/Lock button for a moment and then tap Power Off.) You can use a cloth that's dampened lightly with water, but never use window cleaners, household cleaners, anything from a spray can, alcohol- or ammonia-based cleansers, solvents, or abrasives. Don't get any moisture in your Nexus's openings.

Managing Apps and Services

The Apps screen lets you manage individual apps and services, and change the way your tablet uses memory. To open the Apps screen, tap Settings > Apps. At the top of the Apps screen are three tabs, each showing a list of apps and services. Tap a tab name or swipe left or right to switch tabs:

- **Downloaded.** Lists apps that you've downloaded from Google Play or elsewhere (see "Getting Apps and Games" in Chapter 16).

- **Running.** Lists all apps, processes, and services that are now running or that have cached (temporarily stored) processes, along with how much RAM (memory) they're using . The graph at the bottom of the Running tab shows the total RAM in use and the amount free. To switch lists, tap Show Cached Processes or Show Running Services in the top-right corner of the screen.

A The Running tab of the Apps screen.

Internal Storage and RAM

Apps use two types of memory: internal storage and RAM. Each app, whether it's running or not, uses *internal storage* for itself and its files, settings, and other data. When it's running, each app also uses *RAM* (random access memory) for temporary storage and fast access to some data.

You typically don't need to worry about managing memory yourself. The Nexus's internal storage—where the system files, apps, and most data for those apps are stored—is protected for your privacy. You can't see this part when you connect your Nexus to a computer via a USB cable. The other portion—where music, media, downloaded files, and the like are stored—is visible.

Android also manages how apps use RAM. It usually caches things you've used recently, to enable quick access if you need them again, but it erases the cache if it needs the RAM for new operations. If an app freezes or otherwise jumps the rails, you can monitor its RAM usage and stop it by using the Apps and App Info screens in Settings.

You affect the way that apps use internal storage when you install, use, or delete apps; download, create, or delete files; copy files to or from a computer; and so on. To see how internal storage is being used, tap Settings > Storage.

- **All.** Lists all apps that came with Android and all apps that you downloaded from Google Play or elsewhere **B**.

TIP To sort the lists in the Downloaded or All tab, tap ⋮ > Sort By Name or Sort By Size.

To view details about an app or other item listed in any tab, tap its name. The App Info screen opens **C**.

TIP To open App Info quickly, on the Home screen, tap ⊞ and then drag an app icon to App Info at the top of the screen. (The words *App Info* appear when you drag.) Alternatively, tap ▭, touch and hold an app thumbnail, and then tap App Info.

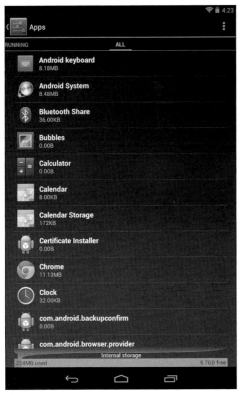

B The All tab of the Apps screen.

C The App Info screen.

The available information and controls vary by item but commonly include the following:

- **Force Stop.** Stops a misbehaving app, service, or process. If your Nexus stops working correctly after a stop, restart your Nexus.

- **Uninstall.** Deletes the app and all its data and settings. You can't uninstall Android's built-in system apps.

- **Uninstall Updates.** Uninstalls all updates to the app, rolling it back to its original version.

- **Disable.** Prevents the app from running but doesn't uninstall it. This option is available for some apps and services that can't be uninstalled.

- **Show Notifications.** Toggles notifications for the app (see Chapter 8).

- **Clear Data.** Deletes an app's settings and other data without removing the app itself.

- **Clear Cache.** Clears any noncrucial data that the app is storing temporarily in memory.

- **Launch by Default.** Lets you change your mind if you've configured an app to launch certain file types by default. You can clear that setting here.

- **Permissions.** Lists the kinds of information about your tablet and the data to which the app has access.

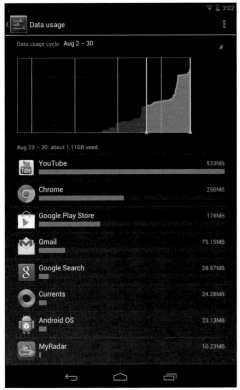

Optimizing Data Usage

To monitor the amount of data uploaded or downloaded by your Nexus during a given period, tap Settings > Data Usage **(A)**. Near the top of the screen is the *data usage cycle,* a date range for which the graph displays data usage. To choose a different cycle, tap the dates. You can drag the vertical white lines on the graph to show a date range within the data usage cycle. This range determines the usage amount displayed in the text message just below the graph.

The list below breaks down data usage by apps and services. Tap an item in the list for more details **B**.

You can reduce data usage by syncing your apps manually and only when you need the data, rather than relying on auto-sync. To toggle autosync, tap ⋮ > Auto-Sync Data. For details, see "Configuring Sync Options" in Chapter 6.

Some apps also let you restrict data usage from the app's own settings, which you can access by tapping View App Settings (if available) **C**.

TIP To identify mobile hotspots and restrict background downloads, tap Settings > Data Usage > ⋮ > Mobile Hotspots. A *mobile hotspot* is typically a smartphone or pocket router sharing its cellular Internet connection wirelessly with nearby devices. Mobile hotspots often have usage caps that carry steep overage charges.

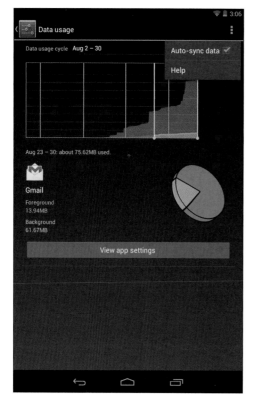

B The Data Usage screen for a specific app. Some apps transfer data in the background when you're not actually using them.

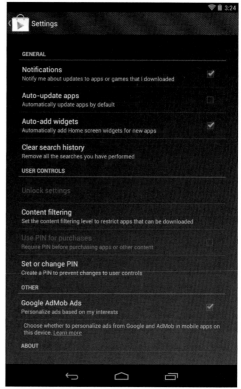

C The Settings screen for a specific app may offer options to restrict that app's data usage.

3

Securing Your Nexus 7

You can use the Nexus 7's security features to protect your data from co-workers, thieves, cops, spouses, lawyers, busybodies, governments, and other snoops.

In This Chapter

Setting the Screen Lock

You can set an automatic screen lock to prevent other people from accessing your Nexus 7. If you set a lock, you must unlock your tablet each time you power on or wake it (see "Powering On and Off" in Chapter 1).

TIP To change when your tablet goes to sleep, tap **Settings > Display > Sleep.**

To set the screen lock:

1. Tap Settings > Security > Screen Lock.

2. Tap the type of lock you want 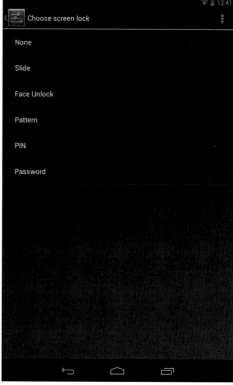, and follow the onscreen instructions.

   If you've previously set a lock, you must enter the pattern, personal identification number (PIN), or password to unlock it.

   The following screen locks are available:

   ▸ **None** disables the screen lock. Waking your Nexus zips you to the screen where you left off.

   ▸ **Slide**, like None, provides no protection, but you must slide a lock icon to dismiss the Lock screen.

Ⓐ The lock options are listed in approximate order of strength, from least secure (None) to most secure (Password).

Face Unlock lets you unlock by looking at the screen (specifically, at the front camera). This lock is fun but not very secure. After you set up Face Unlock, you can strengthen it by tapping Settings > Security and then selecting Improve Face Matching and Liveness Check. The latter option requires you to blink to unlock, thwarting someone from using a photo of you to unlock.

Pattern lets you draw a simple connect-the-dots pattern to unlock.

PIN requires you to type four or more digits to unlock. Longer PINs tend to be more secure.

Password requires you to type four or more characters to unlock **B**.

TIP If your Nexus is playing music when the screen locks, you can continue listening or pause the audio without unlocking.

B The Password option is the most secure lock, provided that you create a strong password—that is, one with at least eight characters, mixing letters, digits, and symbols, and without dictionary words or common phrases.

You can fine-tune the screen lock by setting the following options in the Security screen ⓒ (tap Settings > Security):

- **Automatically Lock.** Locks your tablet a specified amount of time after it goes to sleep. Shorter durations are more secure but less convenient.

- **Power Button Instantly Locks.** Determines whether pressing the Power/Lock button instantly locks the tablet. If this setting is turned off, the tablet locks after the time interval specified by Automatically Lock.

- **Owner Info.** Lets you show owner information or a custom message on the lock screen. If you enter your phone number or email address and then lose your tablet, the finder can contact you without needing to unlock it.

- **Make Passwords Visible.** Displays each PIN or password character briefly as you type it.

TIP To hear a sound when the screen locks or unlocks, tap Settings > Sound > Screen Lock Sound.

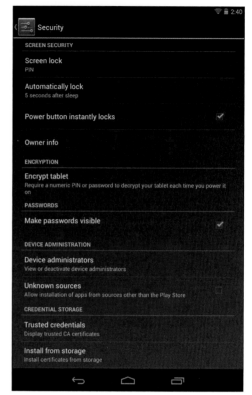

ⓒ You can use the Security screen to tweak screen-lock settings.

Encrypting Your Nexus 7

Setting a PIN or password screen lock is moderately secure, but to stop a determined enemy, you must also encrypt your Nexus 7. Encryption makes data unreadable to anyone without the key and scrambles everything on your tablet: Google Accounts, app data, music and other media, downloaded information, and so on.

Encryption is irreversible. The only way to revert to an unencrypted tablet is to do a factory data reset (tap Settings > Backup & Reset > Factory Data Reset), which erases all data on the tablet.

TIP **If your screen-locked but unencrypted Nexus 7 is stolen, the thief can still read your data by accessing the tablet's internal storage directly, a technically sophisticated but not uncommon procedure.**

To encrypt your Nexus 7:

1. Schedule a free hour for encryption.

   Encryption takes an hour or more, during which time your tablet may restart several times. Don't touch the tablet or interrupt the process; if you do, you'll lose some or all of your data.

2. Set a PIN or Password screen lock.

   For details, see "Setting the Screen Lock" earlier in this chapter.

   The same PIN or password that you use to unlock your tablet is the one you use to encrypt it. You can't set independent screen-unlock and encryption passwords.

continues on next page

3. Charge the battery, and keep the tablet plugged in.

   You can't encrypt unless the tablet is sufficiently charged and plugged into a power source.

4. Tap Settings > Security > Encrypt Tablet.

5. Tap Encrypt Tablet 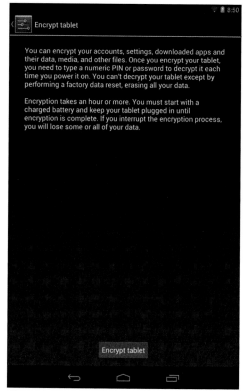.

   If you change your mind about encrypting your tablet, tap the icon in the top-left corner of the screen.

6. Enter your lock-screen PIN or password and then tap Continue.

7. Tap Encrypt Tablet again.

   The encryption process starts and displays its progress.

8. At the prompt when encryption completes, enter your PIN or password.

   From now on, you must enter your PIN or password to decrypt your tablet when you power it on or wake it.

Ⓐ The Encrypt Tablet button is dimmed if your battery isn't charged or your tablet isn't plugged in.

Digital Certificates

You can use *digital certificate* files to identify your Nexus 7 for security purposes. Some organizations use certificates to let mobile devices access private Wi-Fi or VPN networks, or to authenticate certain apps (such as Email or Chrome) to servers. To use a certificate to identify your Nexus, get the certificate file from your system administrator and then install it on your Nexus by following the administrator's instructions. You can manage certificates in the Credential Storage section of the Security screen (tap Settings > Security).

Working with Text

The Nexus isn't all scrolling, dragging, and zooming; it also offers an onscreen keyboard and other tools for working with text. This chapter shows you how to

- Use onscreen or physical keyboards
- Type in other languages
- Cut, copy, and paste text
- Dictate text

In This Chapter

Using the Onscreen Keyboard

An onscreen keyboard  pops up automatically when you tap any area that accepts text. Use the keyboard to type notes, email, messages, Web addresses, passwords, search terms, contact information, or any other text. Typing is straightforward: Tap a character to make it appear in the editing area. The target key turns blue when you tap it.

The onscreen keyboard has much in common with its physical counterpart, plus a few tricks:

- **Keyboard orientation.** The keyboard reorients for portrait (tall) and landscape (wide) views. The latter view is roomier for typing. For details, see "Changing Screen Orientation" in Chapter 2.

- **Uppercase letters.** To type an upper-case letter, tap the Shift key ⇧. This key changes to ⬆ when it's active and then back to normal after you type a letter. To turn on Caps Lock, double-tap or touch and hold ⇧. Tap again to return to lowercase.

- **Character deletion.** To delete the last character that you typed, tap the Backspace key ⌫. To delete multiple characters quickly, touch and hold the Backspace key.

- **Keyboard hiding.** To hide the keyboard, tap the modified Back button ⌄ below the keyboard, or tap off an editable area.

 The Nexus offers alphabetic, numbers-and-punctuation, and symbols keyboards, which you can switch among as you type.

B Touch and hold a key to see whether it offers additional letters or symbols. The E key, for example, lets you type not only the standard e, but also ê, è, é, and other diacriticals.

- **End-of-sentence shortcut.** Double-tap the spacebar at the end of a sentence to end it with a period, move one space to the right, and start the next sentence with an uppercase letter.

- **Accents and diacritical marks.** You can touch and hold certain keys to see variants of their characters in a pop-up box **B**. Slide your finger to the target character in the box and then lift your finger to type it.

- **Alternative key characters.** Some keys have tiny characters in their top-right corners. Touch and hold one of these keys to type its alternative character. Touch and hold the period key ▮, for example, to type a question mark.

- **Keyboard switching.** On the alphabetic keyboard, tap the **?123** key to see numbers and most punctuation. Within that layout, tap the **~\{** key to see less-common symbols, tap **?123** to return to the numbers-and-punctuation layout, or tap **ABC** to return to the alphabetic keys.

- **Momentary keyboard switching.** You can quickly type a character in a different keyboard without switching away from the current one. On the alphabetic keyboard, for example, touch and hold the **?123** key; still touching the screen, slide your finger up to the numeric character that you want; and then lift your finger. Characters are typed only when you lift your finger.

continues on next page

- **Context-sensitive Return key.** The Return key changes to Go, Done, Next, ⬅, or 🔍, depending on whether you're typing ordinary text, a Web or email address, a password, a search term, and so on. If a tiny ellipsis (…) appears on the Return key, you can tap (or touch and hold) the key to jump to the previous or next text field.

- **Web addresses.** When you type a Web address (URL) in Chrome, the Nexus's Web browser, the keyboard includes a .com key. Touch and hold the .com key to get your choice of .net, .org, .edu, and other top-level domains , depending on what country or region you've set your Nexus for.

- **Smileys.** In email, messaging, Chrome, and some other apps, you can tap the :-) key to type a smiley (emoticon) .

C When you're typing a Web address in Chrome, touch and hold the .com key to type a different suffix.

D Emoticons represent facial expressions by using punctuation marks and letters, usually written to express a person's mood. Emoticons are read sideways, most commonly with the eyes on the left, followed by an (optional) nose and then a mouth.

Using Other Input Devices

You can connect joysticks, gamepads, and other input devices to your Nexus. If they work without special drivers or adapters on your computer, they will likely work with your tablet. To take advantage of any special controls (such as dedicated buttons) on an input device, games and apps must be designed explicitly to support them.

Using a Physical Keyboard

If you type a lot of text, work with large documents, or just don't like typing on glass, you can use a physical keyboard. You can connect the keyboard to your Nexus via USB or Bluetooth and then use it just as you would with a computer. For USB connections, you may need an adapter to connect the keyboard to the Nexus's Micro-USB port. To connect a Bluetooth keyboard, see "Bluetooth Devices" in Chapter 5. Bluetooth and unpowered USB connections drain the battery quickly. To connect multiple USB devices, use a powered USB hub.

When you connect a keyboard to your Nexus, you can use it to navigate as well as type text:

- Use the arrow keys to select items.

- Pressing Return when an item is selected is equivalent to tapping that item.

- Pressing Escape is equivalent to tapping Back.

- Pressing Tab or Shift+Tab jumps to the next or previous text field.

Setting Typing Options

The onscreen keyboard has several built-in shortcuts and tricks that you can turn on or off. Tap Settings > Language & Input and then tap next to Android Keyboard. The Android Keyboard Settings screen opens 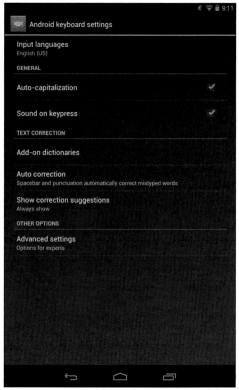 Ⓐ.

> **TIP** You can also open the Android Keyboard Settings screen directly from the keyboard: Tap the key (if it appears) or touch and hold the microphone key 🎤 until the Settings icon appears, and then tap Android Keyboard Settings.

You can set the following options:

- **Auto-Capitalization.** Capitalize the first letter after a period automatically.

- **Sound on Keypress.** Play a sound each time you press a key. To adjust the keypress volume, tap Advanced Settings Ⓐ > Keypress Sound Volume Settings. See also "Adjusting the Volume" in Chapter 2.

- **Add-On Dictionaries.** Install, disable, or delete autocorrection dictionaries for various languages.

> **TIP** Emoji dictionaries add suggestions for smiley faces and other picture characters.

Ⓐ The Android Keyboard Settings screen. After you get the hang of typing on the onscreen keyboard, you'll know whether a particular typing option is helpful or irritating.

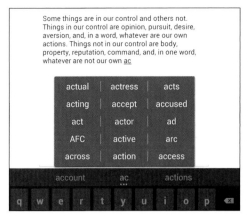

Some things are in our control and others not. Things in our control are opinion, pursuit, desire, aversion, and, in a word, whatever are our own actions. Things not in our control are body, property, reputation, command, and, in one word, whatever are not our own ac

actual	actress	acts
acting	accept	accused
act	actor	ad
AFC	active	arc
across	action	access

account   ac   actions

B Auto Correction suggestions appear at the top of the keyboard as you type. Touch and hold the center suggestion for even more suggestions.

- **Auto Correction.** Suggest words and corrections on the keyboard automatically as you type **B**. In modest mode, tap a suggestion to accept it; to reject it, finish typing the word. In aggressive mode, Auto Correction replaces typos with suggestions automatically when you tap a space or punctuation character at the end of a word. Touch and hold the center suggestion to see additional suggestions.

TIP Auto Correction can make word suggestions based on the last word you typed. To toggle this feature, tap Advanced Settings **A** > Next Word Prediction. While you're on the Advanced Settings screen, you can also toggle whether contact names (from the People app) are suggested.

- **Show Correction Suggestions.** Determines whether Auto Correction suggestions appear.

Checking Spelling

If a misspelled word is flagged with a red underline, tap it to see replacement options **A**. To configure the spell checker, tap Settings > Language & Input > Spell Checker. You can toggle the spell checker or set additional options by tapping ⇌.

Your *personal dictionary* contains a list of words that you don't want to be autocorrected or flagged as misspellings. The dictionary starts out empty. Words are added to it when you tap Add to Dictionary in the spell checker **A**, but you can also edit the dictionary manually: Tap Settings > Language & Input > Personal Dictionary.

Some things are in our control and others not. Things in our control are opinion, pursuit, desire, aversion, and, in a word, whatever are our own actions. Things not in our control are body, properry, reputation, command, and, in one word, ...t our own actions.

property

prepared

prepares

peppered

leopards

+ add to dictionary

× delete

A Tap one of the alternative spellings to replace the misspelled word. If the word you want doesn't appear, just retype it.

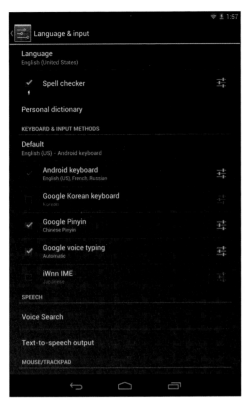

Using International Keyboards

If you communicate in more than one language, you can add keyboards to type in Spanish, Italian, French, German, Chinese, Japanese, Russian, and many more. You can switch keyboards at any time.

TIP The system language, which you chose when you set up your Nexus, is used for the screens, keyboard, and interface. Switching keyboards doesn't affect the system language, which you can view or change by tapping Settings > Language & Input > Language.

To add an international keyboard:

1. Tap Settings > Language & Input to open the Language & Input screen **A**.

A The Language & Input screen. In the Keyboard & Input Methods section, you can toggle keyboards and change their settings by tapping ⊞ next to the keyboard name.

2. To add a Korean, Chinese, or Japanese keyboard, turn on Google Korean Keyboard, Google Pinyin, or iWnn IME.

or

To add keyboards for other languages, tap ⊞ next to Android Keyboard; tap Input Languages; turn off Use System Language; and then select the desired keyboard language(s) **B**.

To switch keyboards:

Tap the Globe key 🌐 repeatedly to cycle through your keyboards. Stop when you see the name of the desired keyboard on the spacebar.

or

Touch and hold the Globe key 🌐, and then tap the desired keyboard in the pop-up list **C**.

B Language variants are listed by country, region, or dialect—English (UK) or French (Canada), for example.

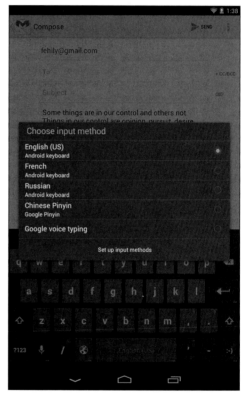

C Go to the globe when you want to switch keyboard languages. The Globe key (next to the spacebar) appears only if you've added multiple keyboards.

The Clipboard

The *clipboard* is the invisible area of memory where the Nexus stores cut or copied content until it's overwritten when you cut or copy something else. This scheme lets you paste the same thing multiple times in different places. You can transfer content from one app to another, provided that the second app can read content generated by the first.

Note that you can't paste something that you've deleted (as opposed to cut), because the Nexus doesn't place the deleted content in the clipboard.

Selecting and Editing Text

The basic text-editing operations are

- **Select.** Highlights text to edit, cut, copy, or format.

- **Cut and paste.** Removes (cuts) content and places it in the clipboard so that it can be moved (pasted) elsewhere. Cutting deletes the content from its original location.

- **Copy and paste.** Copies content to the clipboard so that it can be duplicated (pasted) elsewhere. Copying leaves the original content intact—that is, nothing visible happens.

TIP Apps have no manual **Save** command. Changes are saved automatically every few seconds, or when you switch away from or close the app.

You can select any portion of text within an editable area and then edit it by typing or by using the standard cut, copy, and paste operations.

Selecting and editing text can work differently, depending on which app you're using. In most cases, the rules are

- When you tap text in an editable area, a blinking *insertion point* indicates where new text will appear when you type or paste.

- To move the insertion point, tap near where you want to place it and then drag the blue tab below it 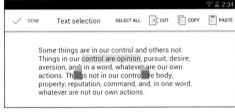. The tab disappears after a few moments; tap again to make it reappear.

- To select text, touch and hold or double-tap it. The nearest word is selected, with a blue tab at each end of the selection. To extend or shorten the range of selected text, drag the tabs to encompass the characters or paragraphs that you want to select. To select all the text in the field or page, tap the Select All button in the top toolbar **B**.

- To cut or copy text, select a range of text and then tap Cut [✂] or Copy [▤] in the top toolbar **B**. To paste text, move the insertion point (or select some text to replace) and then tap Paste [▤], or touch and hold the target area and then tap the Paste button that appears.

TIP In read-only areas—such as in incoming emails and Web pages—the Cut and Paste commands aren't available.

> Some things are in our control and others not. Things in our control are opinion, pursuit, desire, aversion, and in a word, whatever are our own actions. Thi s not in our control are body, property, reputation, command, and, in one word, whatever are not our own actions.

A Drag the blue tab to position the insertion point where you need it to be.

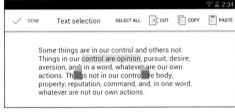

B Toolbar buttons let you select all, cut, copy, or paste text.

Dictating Text

Google Voice Typing lets you dictate text instead of typing on the onscreen keyboard. Dictation works with text areas in any app, without special setup or voice training. (For third-party apps, no additional developer support is required.) To practice, try dictating a message in Gmail.

To turn on and configure dictation:

1. Tap Settings > Languages & Input.

2. To toggle dictation, tap Google Voice Typing.

   When dictation is turned on, the 🎤 key appears on the onscreen keyboard.

3. To configure dictation, tap ⇳ next to Google Voice Typing.

   You can enable other dictation languages, replace naughty words with asterisks, and enable offline dictation.

> **TIP** When you dictate while you're connected to the Internet, what you say is sent to Google's speech-recognition service for conversion to text. Offline dictation is less accurate then online dictation.

To dictate text:

1. Place the insertion point where you want the dictated text to appear.

   Dictation works in most places that you can enter text by using the keyboard.

2. Tap 🎤 on the keyboard and then speak calmly 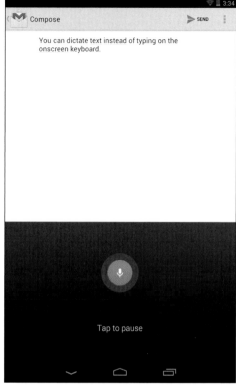.

   The Nexus hears you through its built-in microphone. The 🎤 icon glows to show your speaking volume.

3. When you're finished, tap 🎤 or pause for a few seconds.

   When you pause, what you spoke is transcribed by the speech-recognition service and entered in the text field. You can tap the pop-up Delete button to erase the text (handy for comically wrong transcriptions), or tap underlined text to replace or delete it.

4. To add more text, tap 🎤 again and then continue speaking.

To enter punctuation, say the punctuation mark. Suppose that you want to dictate "Without me, you're nothing." Say this:

Without me comma you're nothing period

Besides punctuation, dictation offers very few commands that let you edit or format text.

🅐 When you're dictating, the onscreen keyboard is replaced by the microphone icon.

Wireless and Network Connections

The Nexus 7 can access the Internet over a Wi-Fi connection. You can jump online from a wireless network at home, work, or school, or from a public Wi-Fi hotspot at a library, café, or airport.

This chapter also covers the Nexus's other wireless features: Bluetooth, VPNs (virtual private networks), and more.

Wi-Fi Connections

Wi-Fi—also known by its less-catchy technical name, *IEEE 802.11*—is the same technology that laptop computers and handheld gadgets use to get online at high speed. After your Nexus is connected to a Wi-Fi network, you can browse the Web, send and receive email, view maps, and do other tasks that require an Internet connection. Wi-Fi also lets you interact with other devices and computers on the same network.

When Wi-Fi is turned on, the Nexus scans continually for nearby networks. You can connect to a Wi-Fi network (and view or change network settings) by tapping Settings > Wi-Fi. When your Nexus is joined to a Wi-Fi network, the Wi-Fi icon 🛜 in the status bar at the top of the screen shows the signal strength. The more bars, the stronger the signal **A**.

You can also connect to a *closed* network—one whose security-minded owner has hidden the network name so that it isn't shown in the list of scanned networks.

Some wireless networks use *MAC address* filtering to restrict access to preapproved computers, devices, and other hardware. To find your Nexus's MAC address, tap Settings > Wi-Fi > ⋮ > Advanced.

After you join a Wi-Fi network, your Nexus automatically reconnects to it whenever the network is in range. If more than one previously used network is in range, your Nexus rejoins the one last used. You can make your Nexus "forget" specific networks (and their passwords) so that it doesn't join them automatically.

Wi-Fi connection and signal-strength indicator

A A glance at the status bar shows your Wi-Fi status.

Login Screens

Many public-access Wi-Fi hotspots don't require a password but do need you to log in or accept terms of use by completing a Web form after you connect. After you join the network, open Chrome, and enter any valid Web address. After a few seconds, a login page should appear if you need to sign in (or pay) for access.

You can also drag down the notification shade from the top of the screen and tap the notification to log in.

Many commercial networks in large public places, such as airports and hotels, charge an hourly or daily fee to your credit card.

B If you're not using the Internet, you can turn off Wi-Fi to conserve battery power.

Lock (indicates that network requires a password) *Signal-strength indicator*

C The Wi-Fi screen lists available Wi-Fi networks and is the gateway to Wi-Fi connections, options, and technical information.

D A secured network requires a password.

If you join a public, unsecured Wi-Fi network, it's easy for the network owner or nearby intruders to collect the unencrypted data (passwords, credit-card numbers, Web addresses, and so on) flowing between your Nexus and the wireless router. Don't shop, bank, or pay bills on such networks. If you have no choice, use a VPN service like WiTopia (https://www.witopia.net).

To turn Wi-Fi on or off:

Tap Settings and then slide the Wi-Fi switch to On or Off **B**.

To connect to a Wi-Fi network:

1. Tap Settings > Wi-Fi.

   The Nexus scans for active Wi-Fi networks within range and lists them **C**. Out-of-range networks to which you've previously connected are listed below in-range networks.

   TIP To scan for networks manually at any time, tap Settings > Wi-Fi > ⋮ > Scan.

2. Tap the name of a network that you want to connect to.

3. If the network is secured, as indicated by a lock icon 🔒, type its password and then tap Connect **D**.

   TIP If your Wi-Fi router supports Wi-Fi Protected Setup, tap the WPS icon and then press the same button on your router.

To forget a network so that your Nexus doesn't join it automatically:

1. Tap Settings > Wi-Fi.

2. Tap the name of the target network.

3. Tap Forget 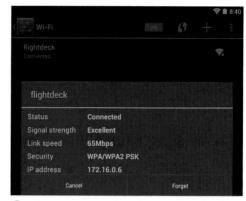.

> **TIP** To forget a network quickly, touch and hold the network name in Settings > Wi-Fi and then tap **Forget Network.**

To join a closed (hidden) Wi-Fi network:

1. Tap Settings > Wi-Fi > ╶┼╴.

2. Enter the network name (SSID), security (encryption) type, and (if required) password ❶.

3. Tap Save.

   The network appears in the Settings > Wi-Fi screen ❸.

To change a network's settings:

1. Tap Settings > Wi-Fi ❸.

2. Touch and hold the network name, and then tap Modify Network to change its settings ❸.

> **TIP** To connect to a network via a proxy server, turn on **Show Advanced Options** when you connect to ❶, add ❶, or modify ❶ a network.

❶ Tap a network name to view or clear its settings.

❶ Before you can join a closed network, the network's owner or administrator must tell you its settings.

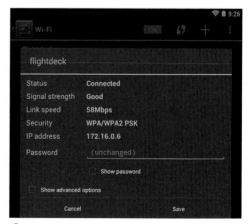

❶ Touch and hold a network name to view or change its settings.

H The Advanced Wi-Fi screen.

Mobile Hotspots

The Nexus 7 can't connect directly to cellular networks—the networks used to make mobile phone calls—but you can still connect to a cellular network over Wi-Fi by using a *mobile hotspot* (a practice also known as *tethering*). A mobile hotspot is a pocket-size gadget or smartphone that offers wireless Internet connections, can connect multiple devices at the same time (like your Nexus, mobile phone, and laptop), and isn't necessarily tied to one carrier.

Sadly, mobile hotspots are expensive, both to buy and to use. For examples, see the Novatel MiFi (http://nvtl.com) or Sierra Wireless AirCard (www.sierrawireless.com). To manage data usage and mobile hotspots, tap Settings > Data Usage > ⁝ > Mobile Hotspots.

To configure general Wi-Fi network settings:

1. Tap Settings > Wi-Fi > ⁝ > Advanced **H**.

2. The following settings and information are available:

   ▸ **Network Notification.** Determines whether you receive notifications in the status bar at the top of the screen when your Nexus detects an open Wi-Fi network.

   ▸ **Keep Wi-Fi on During Sleep.** Determines whether your Nexus stays connected to Wi-Fi when it sleeps. If you're using a mobile hotspot, you can use this option to reduce mobile data usage.

   ▸ **MAC Address.** Shows the Media Access Control (MAC) address of your Nexus when connected to a Wi-Fi network.

   ▸ **IP Address.** Shows the Internet Protocol (IP) address assigned to your Nexus by the Wi-Fi network you're connected to (or your static IP address, if you've set one by tapping Show Advanced Options **H**).

Virtual Private Networks

A *virtual private network* (VPN) lets you connect from your Nexus to an organization's network securely and privately by using the Internet as a conduit. VPN works over Wi-Fi network connections. You can add multiple VPN configurations and switch among them on the VPN screen  (tap Settings > More > VPN).

TIP To use a VPN, you must first set a **PIN** or **Password** screen lock. For details, see "Setting the Screen Lock" in Chapter 3.

To add a new VPN configuration:

1. Tap Settings > More > VPN > Add VPN Profile.

2. Configure the VPN connection based on information you get from your network administrator or your organization's IT department **B**.

3. Tap Save.

   The VPN is added to the list on the VPN screen **A**.

To connect to a VPN:

1. Tap Settings > More > VPN **A**.

2. Tap the name of the VPN.

3. In the screen that opens, enter your credentials **C**.

4. Tap Connect.

   While you're connected to a VPN, a status-bar icon and notification are displayed. To disconnect, tap the notification for the VPN connection.

A The VPN screen.

B If you've set up a VPN on your computer, you may be able to use the same VPN settings for your Nexus.

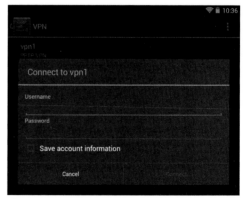

C If you don't want to type your credentials every time you connect, turn on Save Account Information.

Bluetooth Devices

Bluetooth is a wireless technology that provides short-range (up to 32 feet/ 10 meters) radio links between a Nexus and external keyboards, headphones, speakers, or other Bluetooth-equipped devices. It eliminates cable clutter while simplifying communications, sharing, and data synchronization between devices. Bluetooth doesn't need a line-of-sight connection, so you can, say, use a hands-free headset to listen to music playing on the Nexus in your backpack.

A *passcode* (or personal identification number [PIN]) is a number that associates your Nexus with a Bluetooth device. For security, many Bluetooth devices make you use a passcode to ensure that your Nexus is connecting to your device and not someone else's nearby. Check the device's manual for a passcode. (The most common passcodes are 0000 and 1234.)

Before you can use a Bluetooth device, you must make it *discoverable* and then pair it with your Nexus; the device will come with instructions. *Pairing* (or *passcode exchange*) gets the Nexus to positively identify the device that you want to connect to. After it's paired, the device autoconnects whenever it's within range of your Nexus. You can pair your Nexus with multiple devices at the same time (say, a headset and a keyboard).

Your Nexus comes with a generic Bluetooth name, visible to other Bluetooth devices when you connect them. You can change the name to something more meaningful.

To turn Bluetooth on or off:

Tap Settings and then slide the Bluetooth switch to On or Off **A**.

When Bluetooth is on, a Bluetooth icon ✳ appears in the status bar at the top of the screen.

To change your Nexus's Bluetooth name:

1. Make sure Bluetooth is turned on.

2. Tap Settings > Bluetooth > ⋮ > Rename Tablet.

To pair a Bluetooth device with your Nexus:

1. On your Nexus, make sure Bluetooth is turned on.

2. Turn on your Bluetooth device and then follow the instructions that came with it to make it discoverable.

3. On your Nexus, tap Settings > Bluetooth **B**.

   The Bluetooth screen lists nearby discoverable devices. If you don't see your device, tap Search for Devices at the top of the screen.

4. Tap the Bluetooth name of your Nexus near the top of the Bluetooth screen to make it visible to all nearby Bluetooth devices.

> **TIP** To change the amount of time that your Nexus remains visible, tap ⋮ > **Visibility Timeout.**

A If you're not connected to a Bluetooth device, you can turn off Bluetooth to conserve battery power.

B The Bluetooth screen.

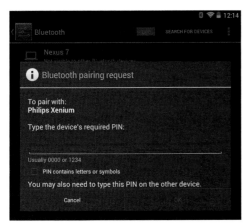

C If requested, type the passcode (PIN) to complete the pairing. (Check the device's manual for the passcode.)

5. Tap the device in the Available Devices list and then follow the onscreen instructions **C**.

After you've paired with a Bluetooth device, you can connect to it manually (to switch devices, for example, or to reconnect after it's back in range).

TIP Some Bluetooth audio devices come with a small separate transceiver that plugs into the Nexus's headset jack. If you have one of these transceivers, you don't need to turn on Bluetooth; the plug-in takes care of the connection.

To connect to a Bluetooth device:

1. Make sure Bluetooth is turned on.

2. Tap Settings > Bluetooth **B**.

3. In the list of devices, tap a paired but unconnected device.

When the Nexus and the device are connected, the device is shown as connected in the list.

TIP If you transfer files to your Nexus via Bluetooth, you can see them by tapping ⋮ > Show Received Files.

To unpair, rename, or configure a paired Bluetooth device:

1. Make sure Bluetooth is turned on.

2. Tap Settings > Bluetooth **B**.

3. Tap ⊟ next to the device name.

Android Beam

Android Beam lets you easily share your photos, videos, contacts, Web pages, YouTube videos, directions, apps, and other content with a simple tap. Touch your Nexus 7 to another Android device (smartphone or tablet) back to back and then tap to beam whatever's on your screen to your friend's device (or vice versa).

Both devices must be NFC-enabled to use Android Beam. *NFC* (Near Field Communication) lets devices establish radio communication with each other when they're touching or in close proximity. The Nexus 7 supports NFC. If the other device doesn't support NFC, you can't use Android Beam.

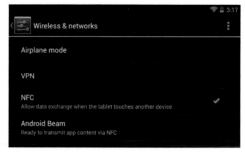

Ⓐ NFC and Android Beam must be enabled on both devices.

To beam screen content:

1. Make sure NFC is enabled on both devices.

   To enable NFC on your Nexus 7, tap Settings > More and then select the NFC check box Ⓐ.

2. Make sure Android Beam is enabled on both devices.

   To enable Android Beam on your Nexus 7, tap Settings > More > Android Beam > On.

3. Open a screen containing what you want to share (photo, video, map, whatever).

4. Move the back of your Nexus 7 toward the back of the other device.

   When the devices connect, you hear a sound, and your screen image shrinks and shows the message *Touch to beam*.

TIP For best results, touch the other device to the back of your Nexus 7 near the *u* in *nexus*.

5. Tap your screen anywhere.

   The open app determines what's beamed. Your friend's device displays the transferred content.

   or

   If the necessary app isn't installed, Google Play opens to a screen where your friend can download the app.

TIP You can also instantly pair your Nexus to Bluetooth devices (like headsets or speakers) that support the Simple Secure Pairing standard just by tapping the devices together.

Airplane Mode

If an airplane's cabin crew asks you to turn off electronic devices to avoid interfering with the flight instruments, tap Settings > More > Airplane Mode 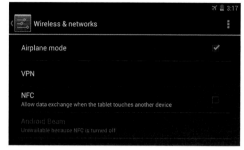 to suppress your Nexus's Wi-Fi, Bluetooth, NFC, GPS, and other wireless signals. You can still play downloaded music and videos, read books, and do other non-Internet things. When airplane mode is on, ✈ appears in the status bar at the top of the screen.

If the plane offers in-flight Wi-Fi, tap Settings > Wi-Fi > On. If you're using a Bluetooth accessory, tap Settings > Bluetooth > On.

When you're not using the Internet, airplane mode is also a quick way to turn off all your Nexus's battery-draining wireless services in one shot.

Ⓐ Airplane mode turns off all data transmission from your Nexus.

Managing Your Accounts and Data

When you first set up your Nexus 7, you created a Google Account or signed in to an existing one. (If you skipped that step, this chapter shows you how.) If you have multiple Google Accounts, you can add them all. The Nexus also supports third-party accounts for Internet-based mail and other online services, such as Yahoo, Microsoft Exchange, and Skype. Moreover, you can sync (synchronize) some or all data associated with accounts, ensuring that information is kept up to date in multiple locations (such as on the Web and locally on your Nexus). For Google Accounts, online backups let you restore your data and settings to any Android tablet or smartphone.

In This Chapter

Adding and Removing Accounts

You can add, edit, and remove accounts by using the Accounts section of the Settings screen . By default, Settings lets you add Google, Microsoft Exchange, and Web-based email accounts. You can add other types of accounts, depending on which apps you've installed. Accounts for some apps—such as Skype, Facebook, Twitter, and Dropbox—appear in Settings only after you sign in to the app directly. In other apps, such as Amazon Kindle, you manage your account entirely within the app, without tapping Settings > Accounts.

Adding accounts typically is painless, but for some accounts, you may need to get details from the system administrator or service provider. Most accounts request a username and password, but depending on the service you're connecting to, you may also have to provide a domain or server address.

To add an account:

1. Tap Settings > Accounts to open the Accounts screen Ⓐ.

2. Tap ╋ Add Account.

3. In the Add an Account dialog box Ⓑ, tap the type of account to add.

   To add a Google Account, tap Google. To add a Microsoft Exchange account, tap Corporate. To add a Web-based mail account, tap Email. Other types of accounts may also be available, depending on which apps you've installed.

Ⓐ The Accounts section of the Settings screen shows accounts that you're signed in to.

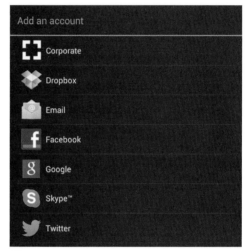

Ⓑ The list of available account types depends on which apps you've installed.

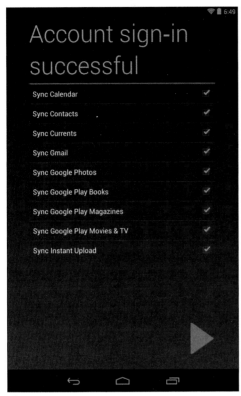

Account sign-in
successful

Sync Calendar

Sync Contacts

Sync Currents

Sync Gmail

Sync Google Photos

Sync Google Play Books

Sync Google Play Magazines

Sync Google Play Movies & TV

Sync Instant Upload

C Depending on the kind of account, you may be asked to name the account, specify which data to sync (as shown here for a Google Account), and supply other details.

4. Follow the onscreen instructions, which vary by account type **C**.

   When you're done, the account is added to the Accounts screen **A**.

TIP You can also add a Google or email account from directly within the Gmail or Email app, either in the initial screen or the screen that results from tapping ⁝ > Settings.

To edit an account:

1. Tap Settings > Accounts to open the Accounts screen **A**.

2. Tap the account type, and then, if necessary, tap the account name.

   You can view or change the account's current settings, which vary by account.

To remove an account:

1. Tap Settings > Accounts **A**.

2. Tap the account type, and then, if necessary, tap the account name.

3. Tap ⁝ > Remove Account.

   All information associated with the account (email, contacts, settings, and so on) is removed as well.

TIP For some types of accounts, the ⁝ > Remove Account command isn't available, In that case, look for a Remove option in the Accounts screen or within the app itself.

Configuring Sync Options

You can configure sync options for any of your apps and decide what kinds of data to sync for each account.

If an account does *two-way sync,* changes that you make to the information on your Nexus are also applied to the copy of that information on the Web, and vice versa. Most accounts, including Google Accounts, work this way. Changes that you make in the People app on your Nexus, for example, are made automatically to your Google contacts on the Web. If an account does only *one-way sync,* the information on your Nexus is read-only.

TIP **Some apps let you fine-tune sync settings within the app. In Gmail, for example, tap ⋮ > Manage Labels, tap a label, and then tap Sync Messages.**

You can sync manually or automatically by using the autosync feature. To toggle autosync, tap Settings > Data Usage > ⋮ > Auto-Sync Data. If autosync is turned off, you won't receive notifications when updates occur; you must sync manually (using the app's own tools) to collect recent email, messages, and so on. Sync options vary by account type; this section shows you how to configure Google Account sync settings. For other accounts, tap the account name in the Settings > Accounts screen to see what's available.

TIP **If you don't need to sync automatically, you can turn off autosync to conserve battery power.**

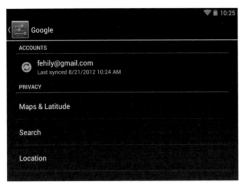

A The Google screen lists your Google Accounts and their sync status.

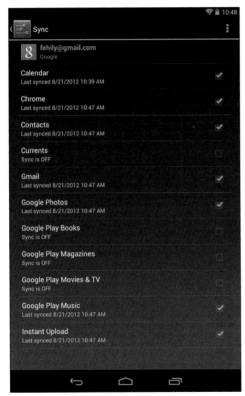

B The Sync screen for a Google Account.

To set sync options for a Google Account:

1. Tap Settings > Google (below Accounts).

   The Google screen opens **A**. Near the top of the screen, each Google Account is listed, along with the time of its most recent sync (if applicable). The color of the sync icon ⟳ indicates the sync status: green = OK, red = error, and gray = off.

2. Tap the account whose sync settings you want to change.

   The Sync screen opens **B**.

3. Tap items to select or clear their check boxes.

   Clearing an item doesn't remove information from your Nexus; it simply stops it from syncing with the version on the Web.

To sync a Google Account manually:

1. Tap Settings > Google (below Accounts) **A**.

2. Tap the account whose data you want to sync **B**.

3. Tap ⋮ > Sync Now.

Backing Up or Erasing Your Data

You can back up settings and other data associated with your Google Account(s). If you replace your Nexus 7 or get a new Android gadget, you can restore your data for any account that you previously backed up. You can also reset your Nexus to its original factory state, erasing all your personal data and settings (handy if you're selling your Nexus).

Tap Settings > Backup & Reset and then tap one of the following options in the Backup & Reset screen 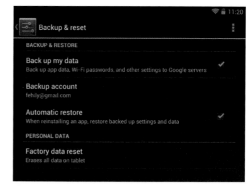:

- **Back Up My Data.** Backs up a variety of your personal data, including Wi-Fi passwords, Chrome bookmarks, Google Play apps, personal-dictionary words, Home-screen layout, and most of your custom settings. Some third-party apps tap into this feature, so you can restore your data if you reinstall an app.

  If you turn off this option, your data is no longer backed up, and any existing back-ups are deleted from Google's servers.

- **Backup Account.** Lists which Google Accounts are backed up. To back up additional accounts, tap Backup Account > Add Account.

> **TIP** You can restore only a backed-up account when you factory-reset or first set up your Nexus. (See "Setting Up Your Nexus 7" in Chapter 1.)

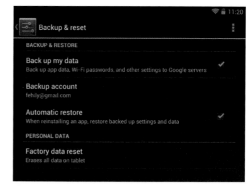

Ⓐ The Backup & Reset screen.

- **Automatic Restore.** Restores an app's data and settings when you reinstall the app, provided that the app supports the backup service.

- **Factory Data Reset.** Erases all your personal data and settings from your Nexus, including your Google Account; other accounts; system and app settings; network settings; downloaded apps; and your media, documents, and other files. Charge the battery before a reset. After resetting your Nexus, you must go through the setup process again. (See "Setting Up Your Nexus 7" in Chapter 1.)

Connecting to Computers

You can use the USB cable that came with your Nexus 7 to transfer files to and from your Windows PC or Macintosh computer.

Connecting to a Windows PC via USB

You can use a USB cable to connect your Nexus 7 to a Windows computer and transfer music, videos, pictures, documents, and other files between them. This connection uses Media Transfer Protocol (MTP). Windows Vista, Windows 7, and later support MTP. Windows XP supports MTP only if Windows Media Player 10 or later is installed. Pre-XP versions of Windows may not recognize the Nexus 7.

When you connect your Nexus to a USB port on your computer, the message *Connected as a media device* flashes briefly in the Nexus's status bar at the top of the screen. In Windows, the Nexus's USB storage appears as a drive in the Computer folder Ⓐ. To open the Computer folder on your PC, choose Start > Computer or press Windows logo key + E. Double-click the Nexus 7 folder and its subfolders to navigate its internal storage Ⓑ.

You can copy files back and forth as you would using any other external storage device. If you copy a folder of photos from your computer to the Nexus's internal storage, for example, you can view it as an album in the Gallery app. When you're done, disconnect the USB cable.

> **TIP** To change your Nexus's USB connection options, tap Settings > Storage > ⋮ > USB Computer Connection.

Ⓐ The Computer folder in Windows.

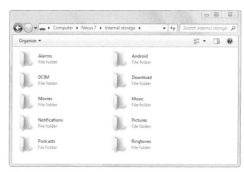

Ⓑ Double-click folders to burrow to the file or folder you want. To return the previous folder, press Backspace or click the Back button in the toolbar.

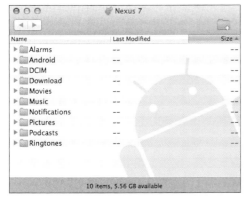

A You work with the Android File Transfer window much as though it were a Finder window.

Connecting to a Mac via USB

You can use a USB cable to connect your Nexus 7 to a Macintosh computer and transfer music, videos, pictures, documents, and other files between them. This connection uses Media Transfer Protocol (MTP). Mac OS X doesn't support MTP natively, so you must first install the free Android File Transfer application on your Mac: Go to www.android.com/filetransfer, and then follow the download and installation instructions.

The first time that you use Android File Transfer, double-click it to open it. Afterward, it opens automatically when you connect your Nexus 7 to your Mac via USB cable.

When you connect your Nexus to a USB port on your computer, the message *Connected as a media device* flashes briefly in the Nexus's status bar at the top of the screen. On your Mac, Android File Transfer opens a window that displays the contents of your Nexus 7, along with storage-space details at the bottom of the window **A**.

You can copy files back and forth as you would using any other external storage device. If you copy a folder of photos from your computer to the Nexus's internal storage, for example, you can view it as an album in the Gallery app. When you're done, disconnect the USB cable.

TIP To change your Nexus's USB connection options, tap Settings > Storage > ⁞ > USB Computer Connection.

8

Getting Notifications

Certain apps can push notifications to you even when you're not actively using those apps. The Nexus 7 provides a central list, called the *notification shade,* of all the apps that are trying to get your attention. You can get notifications for incoming mail and messages, calendar events, alarms, ongoing or completed downloads, system and app updates, and more. The Nexus's built-in apps, as well as third-party apps, can send notifications.

In This Chapter

Viewing Notifications

When a notification arrives, its icon appears in the status bar at the top of the screen **A**. To open the notification shade, swipe down from the top of the screen **B**. To close the notification shade, tap off the shade or swipe up from the bottom of the shade.

Pending notifications

A The status bar alerts you to new notifications.

Lock/unlock screen rotation. *Open Settings.*

Dismiss all notifications.

Tap to take a specific action.

Spread or pinch to expand or collapse.

Tap icon to open associated app.

Swipe left or right to dismiss notification.

B The notification shade lists recent notifications.

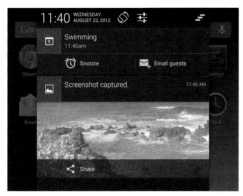

A Notifications in expanded...

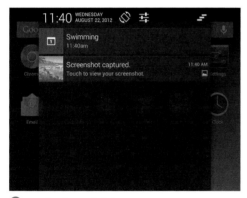

B ...and collapsed states.

Managing Notifications

Here are some tips for using notifications:

- The icons at the top of the shade offer shortcuts to common features. Tap ◇ to toggle the screen rotation lock (see "Changing Screen Orientation" in Chapter 2) or tap ⊡ to open the Settings app (see "Viewing and Changing Settings" in Chapter 1).

- To open the app that sent the notification, tap the notification icon or image on the left side of the shade. (In some cases, such as email notifications, you can tap any part of the notification.)

- Some notifications can be expanded to show more information, such as email previews, pictures, or calendar events. The topmost notification is always expanded, if possible. You can swipe two fingers or spread or pinch to expand **A** or collapse **B** a notification.

Some expanded notifications contain icons that let you take certain actions from within the notification itself. Calendar notifications, for example, let you snooze (remind you later) or send email to other guests.

continues on next page

- When you're done with a notification, swipe it left or right to dismiss it. To dismiss all notifications, tap ⬛ at the top of the shade. A notification will also self-dismiss when you tap it to jump to its related app.

- You can set notification preferences in individual apps, typically by tapping ⋮ > Settings in the app ⓒ.

- To change the alert sound for new notifications, tap Settings > Sound > Default Notification.

- To set the volume of the notification sound (separately from the main volume), tap Settings > Sounds > Volumes.

ⓒ Notification settings in the Gmail app.

9

Google Now

Google Now is a personalized search app that recognizes your repeated actions on your tablet and displays relevant information when you summon it.

In This Chapter

Using Google Now

Google Now uses a wide array of personal and public data—including your current location, commonly visited places, calendar events, and search history—to provide contextually relevant information when you need it. When you have a meeting, for example, Google Now automatically offers directions to the location and travel time in current traffic conditions.

To open Google Now **A**, swipe up from the bottom of the screen, or tap the Google app in the Home or All Apps screen.

> **TIP** If you're using the Slide screen lock, you can open Google Now by dragging the lock icon straight up to the word *Google* on the lock screen. (See "Setting the Screen Lock" in Chapter 3.)

You can fine-tune some settings by tapping ⋮ > Settings at the bottom of the Google Now screen, but the best way to customize it is to simply be you. Commute to work. Walk around town. Search the Web. Make appointments. Check the weather. Compare flights. Look up sports scores. Travel. Do the things that you normally do. Over time, Google Now learns your habits and interests, and shows you contextual information based on your calendar, recent searches, current location, or time of day, sometimes in surprising ways. If you're near a subway stop in New York City, for example, Google Now shows you what trains are coming next, when they'll arrive, and where they're headed. If you're traveling internationally, currency-exchange rates appear.

> **TIP** Google Now is integrated with Google Search. For details on using the search bar at the top of the Google Now screen, see Chapter 10.

A Google Now.

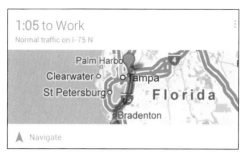

A A Google Now card.

B The Google Now sample-cards screen.

Displaying and Managing Cards

Google Now displays each snippet of information as a discrete card A that slides into view when Google Now thinks you're likely to need it.

When Google Now has a new update, a notification appears in the status bar at the top of the screen. You can drag the notification shade down from the top of the screen to see the card or dismiss the notification. For details, see Chapter 8.

You can show more cards, browse sample cards, dismiss cards, and edit card settings.

To show more cards:

Scroll to the bottom of the Google Now screen and then tap Show More Cards.

After you tap Show More Cards, the option name changes to Show Sample Cards.

To browse sample cards:

1. Scroll to the bottom of the Google Now screen and then tap Show Sample Cards to open the sample-cards screen B.

   If Show Sample Cards isn't visible, tap ⋮ > Sample Cards.

   continues on next page

2. Scroll the list to see all the cards and then tap a Sample Card link to see that sample card .

3. When you're done, scroll to the bottom of the screen and then tap Hide Sample Cards.

To dismiss a card:

■ Scroll the Google Now screen to the target card and then swipe the card left or right.

The card returns the next time it's relevant, which may be minutes, hours, or days from now.

To edit card settings:

1. In the Google Now screen, tap ⋮ > Settings on the target card.

or

Scroll to the bottom of the Google Now screen and then tap ⋮ > Settings > Google Now **D** > *card name*.

or

In the sample-cards screen **B**, tap Settings on the target card.

C A sample card.

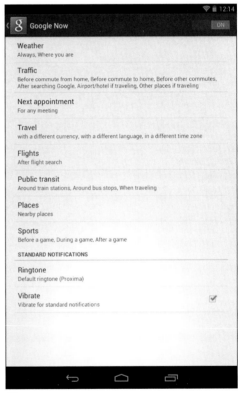

D The settings screen for Google Now lists available cards and synopses of their current settings.

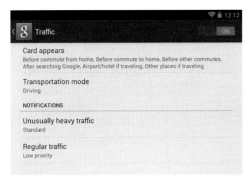

E Settings for the Traffic card.

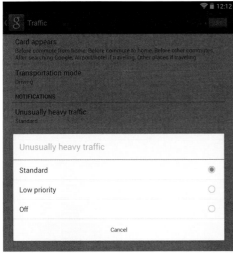

F Notification settings for the Traffic card.

2. Set the options E, which vary by card.

To turn a card on or off, tap the On/Off slider in the top-right corner.

Notifications for most cards can be turned off or set to low or standard priority F. Low-priority notifications appear at the bottom of the notification shade with no additional signal. Standard notifications appear like the others, in chronological order.

TIP You can set the ringtone (alert sound) and vibration for standard notifications in the Google Now settings screen D.

Changing Home and Work Locations

Some Google Now cards, such as Traffic, offer traffic information and travel help. If you commute to and from work daily, Google Now usually can figure out your home and work locations, but it's surer to enter them manually.

To change your home and work locations manually:

When a Traffic card for home or work appears in Google Now, tap ⋮ (on the card) > Edit 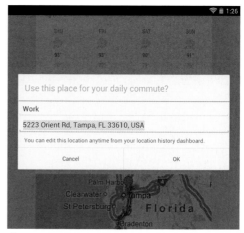.

or

Open the Latitude app, tap ⊙ to find your current location, tap your name on the map, and then tap Location History > Change Home Location or Change Work Location.

or

In a browser, go to https://maps.google.com, tap My Places, and then tap Home or Work.

or

In a browser, go to https://google.com/locationhistory, tap Dashboard, and then tap Change next to Time at Work or Time at Home.

TIP If you visit a Google Web site from a different device or computer, make sure that you're signed in to the same Google Account that you use on your Nexus.

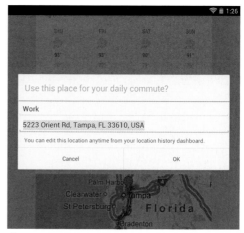

A You can change your work or home address if you move or find a new job, or if Google Now guesses wrong.

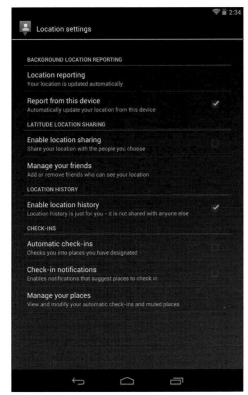

Ⓐ The Location Settings screen in Google Maps.

Controlling Location Privacy

If Google Now's location tracking feels Big Brotherish, you can turn off location reporting and history and still use Google Now, but location and traffic information will be limited or won't appear.

Even if you turn off both location reporting and history, your previously recorded history is still available to Google Now and other Google products unless you delete it manually.

If you're feeling very private—you know who you are—you can turn off Google's Location Services and GPS to stop your Nexus from reporting location data to various apps, though doing so will disable many useful features on your Nexus.

To turn off location reporting and history:

1. Scroll to the bottom of the Google Now screen and then tap ⁞ > Settings > Privacy and Accounts > Manage Location History.

   The Settings screen for Google Maps opens.

2. If necessary, sign in to Google Maps.

3. Tap Location Settings to open the screen of the same name Ⓐ.

4. To turn off location reporting, tap Location Reporting and then select Do Not Update Your Location.

5. To turn off location history, clear the Enable Location History check box.

To delete your location history:

In a browser, go to https://maps.google.com/locationhistory, sign in if necessary, tap Map, and then tap Delete All History .

TIP If you visit a Google Web site from a **different device or computer, make sure that you're signed in to the same Google Account that you use on your Nexus.**

B The Location History Web page lets you delete your location history, as well as view your history for any date. You can also delete a portion of your location history, starting from a specific date you choose in the calendar.

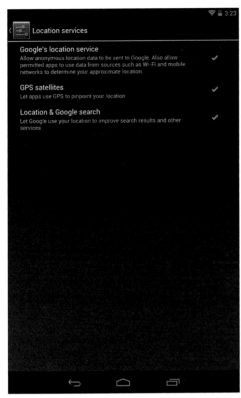

G The Location Services screen.

To turn off location services and GPS:

1. Scroll to the bottom of the Google Now screen and then tap ⋮ > Settings > Privacy and Accounts > Location Services.

   The Location Services screen opens **G**.

2. Tap to clear the check boxes titled Google's Location Service and GPS Satellites.

TIP See also "Using Location Services" in Chapter 17.

Turning Off Google Now

You can turn Google Now (and your location history) off at any time. Scroll to the bottom of the Google Now screen and then tap ⋮ > Settings > Google Now > On/Off slider (at the top of the screen).

Turning off Google Now stops the display of cards and returns Google Now settings to their defaults.

10

Google Search

Google Search lets you search the Web, search your tablet, and issue commands, all by typing or speaking.

Using Google Search

Google Search on your Nexus offers all the features of Google.com on the Web, plus extras such as voice search, audible feedback, and the ability to search your tablet. You can also use voice actions to get directions, send email, and issue other Android commands.

The search bar is available at

- The top of the Home screen .
- The top of the Google Now screen. (Swipe up from the bottom of the screen to open Google Now.)
- The top of the Chrome browser app.

To search by typing:

1. Tap the search bar.

   The onscreen keyboard appears. (For typing tips, see Chapter 4.)

2. Type your query in the search box.

   As you type, suggestions appear below the search box **B**. The first few suggestions try to complete what you're typing.

3. To search for a suggestion immediately, tap it.

   or

   To search for the contents of the search box, tap the Search key 🔍 on the keyboard.

To search (voice search) or issue commands (voice actions) by speaking:

1. Tap the microphone icon 🎤 in the search bar **A**.

   or

   Tap the search bar in the Home screen and then say "Google".

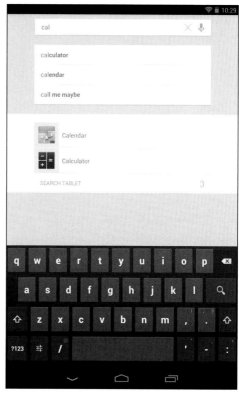

A The search bar is available throughout Android.

B Tap a suggestion to search the Web by using Google, or tap one of the lower results to search your tablet.

C Speak when the microphone icon appears.

D Web searches show a conventional list of Google search results. Some results also show a card and produce an audible response ("It's 53 degrees and partly cloudy in San Francisco"). If you like, you can swipe the card out of the way.

or

On the Google Now screen, say "Google". (You don't have to tap the search bar—just speak.)

or

 Tap the Voice Search app on the Home Screen or the All Apps screen.

TIP Search uses *hotword detection* to trigger a search or action when you say "Google". To turn it off or on, swipe up from the bottom of the screen to open Google Now and then tap ⁝ > **Settings** > **Voice** > **Hotword Detection**.

2. Speak the terms to search for or the voice action to perform C.

For conventional Web searches (voice search), results are listed and, in some cases, read aloud D. For commands (voice actions), the related app opens or a card appears that you can tap to complete the command E.

TIP Only spoken searches, not typed ones, produce audible responses.

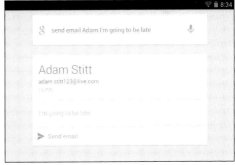

E Voice actions are triggered by certain phrases (covered later in this chapter) such as "Send email" and "Directions to".

Running Sample Search Queries

The best way to learn about Google Search is to experiment. Here are some sample queries to get you started:

- "New York Yankees" **A** (or any team name)
- "Pictures of New Zealand" **B** (or "Images of New Zealand")
- "Convert 100 miles to kilometers" **C**

  You can convert standard units of measure, including distances, temperatures, angles, areas, astronomical units, cooking measures, time periods, energy, density, pressure, speed, volume, weight/mass, power, frequency, and more.

A Result card for "New York Yankees".

B Result card for "Pictures of New Zealand".

100 miles = **160.9344 kilometers**

Source: google.com
Read more

C Result card for "Convert 100 miles to kilometers".

- "The Dark Knight Rises Miami" **D** (or simply "Movie" or *"movie name"* for local movie showtimes)
- "Define schadenfreude" **E**
- "Weather Dublin" **F** (or simply "Weather" for the local weather)
- "Area code 808"
- "Zip code 97201" (or "Postal code 97201")
- "Time in Paris" **G** (or simply "Time" for the local time)

continues on next page

D Results for "The Dark Knight Rises Miami".

scha·den·freu·de
/ˈSHädən ˌfroidə/

Noun: Pleasure derived by someone from another person's misfortune

Wikipedia   Dictionary.com
Answers.com   Merriam-Webster

E Result card for "Define schadenfreude".

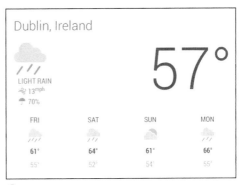

F Results for "Weather Dublin".

9:03pm

Paris, France

G Result card for "Time in Paris".

- "United Airlines Flight 824"

- "Translate to German A beer please"

  You can translate to many other languages.

- "80 divided by 6 plus 7"

  You can use any mathematical expression.

- "Chinese food in Ann Arbor, Michigan"

  Or you can simply say *"food name"* for the local restaurants and markets.

United Airlines
flight 824

Status: On-time / Fri, Aug 24, 2012

Depart Kahului
OGG 11:58 AM
     Gate 27

Arrive San Francisco
SFO 7:35 PM (7:55 PM)
     Terminal 3, Gate 82

Status: On-time / Fri, Aug 24, 2012

Depart San Francisco
SFO 10:33 PM (10:30 PM)
     Terminal 3

Arrive New York
JFK 6:29am, Sat, Aug 25 (6:59 AM)
     Terminal 7

Result card for "United Airlines Flight 824".

$(80 / 6) + 7 = 20.3333333$

Source: google.com
Read more

Result card for "80 divided by 6 plus 7".

A	Lucky Kitchen 1753 Plymouth Road, Ann Arbor
B	San Fu 625 South Main Street, Ann Arbor
C	TK WU Restaurant 510 East Liberty Street, Ann Arbor
D	Gourmet Garden 2255 West Stadium Boulevard, Ann Arbor
E	Middle Kingdom 332 South Main Street, Ann Arbor
F	China Gate Restaurant 1201 South University Avenue, Ann Arbor
G	Evergreen Restaurant 2771 Plymouth Road, Ann Arbor

Result card for "Chinese food in Ann Arbor, Michigan".

Google Inc
NASDAQ: GOOG - Aug 24 3:32pm ET

679.00   +2.20 (0.33%)

OPEN	675.60	VOLUME	1,043,539
HIGH	680.45	AVG VOL	2,290,000
LOW	674.08	MKT CAP	222.06B

Disclaimer

K Result card for "Google stock price".

David Fincher

Director of Fight Club

Source: wikipedia.org
Image: wikipedia.org   Read more

L Result card for "Who directed Fight Club".

Christopher Marlowe

Author of The Tragical History of Doctor Faustus

Source: wikipedia.org
Image: listal.com   Read more

M Result card for "Who wrote Doctor Faustus".

- "Google stock price" **K**
- "Who directed Fight Club" **L**
- "Who wrote Doctor Faustus" **M**
- "What year was The Call of the Wild published" **N**
- "What year was the Eiffel Tower built"
- "What is the second law of thermodynamics" **O**
- "How many protons are in carbon"

continues on next page

1903...

...according to these web pages

N Result card for "What year was The Call of the Wild published".

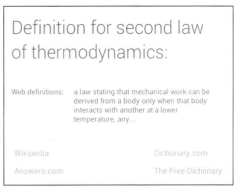

Definition for second law of thermodynamics:

Web definitions: a law stating that mechanical work can be derived from a body only when that body interacts with another at a lower temperature; any...

Wikipedia   Dictionary.com

Answers.com   The Free Dictionary

O Result card for "What is the second law of thermodynamics".

- "What is the speed of light in parsecs per year"
- "Who invented the carburetor"
- "Where is Old Faithful"

the speed of light = 0.30659458
Parsecs per year

Source: google.com
Read more

P Result card for "What is the speed of light in parsecs per year".

Donát Bánki, János Csonka

Q Result card for "Who invented the carburetor".

A   Yellowstone National Park
200, Wyoming

B   Old Faithful Inn
In Old Faithful Inn, WY

C   Grant Village
1 Grand Loop Road, Yellowstone National Park, WY 82190

R Result card for "Where is Old Faithful".

Using Voice Actions

You can use voice actions with Google Search to get directions, send email, and issue other common commands. Search distinguishes voice actions from conventional search terms by listening for special phrases that trigger commands, listed in **Table 10.1**. If Search doesn't understand you, it lists a set of possible meanings; tap the one you want.

Some voice actions, such as "Send email" and "Note to self", open a panel that lets you complete the action by typing or speaking. (For the latter, see "Dictating Text" in Chapter 4.).You can tap any existing text in the panel to edit it. Tap or drag across underlined words to see a list of alternative transcriptions. (Search underlines words that it didn't hear clearly.) Buttons at the bottom of the panel let you add optional fields or complete the action.

TABLE 10.1 Voice Actions Commands

Say	Followed By	Examples
"Map of"	Address, point of interest, landmark, business name, type of business, or other location (see Chapter 17)	"Map of Ann Arbor, Michigan" "Map of Microsoft, Redmond, Washington" "Map of Hyde Park, London" "Map of Cuban restaurants, Miami" "Map of Yosemite Park" "Map of my location"
"Directions to" *or* "Navigate to"	Address, point of interest, landmark, business name, type of business, or other destination (see Chapter 17)	"Directions to Delano Hotel, Miami Beach" "Navigate to 1000 Fifth Avenue, New York City" "Navigate to home" "Directions to work"
"Go to"	Web address (URL) or search string	"Go to google.com"
"Send email"	One or more of the following: "To" and contact names "Cc" and contact names "Bcc" and contact names "Subject" and subject text "Message" and message text (speak punctuation) (See Chapter 15 for more on email.)	"Send email to Sally Ott, subject, Just a reminder, message, Without me comma you're nothing period"
"Note to self"	Email message text	"Note to self Return signed contract"
"Set alarm"	"For", time, "Label" and name of alarm	"Set alarm for 8:30 a.m." "Set alarm for 15 minutes from now" "Set alarm for 6 p.m., label, park concert"
"Listen to"	Words to search Play Music or YouTube for, such as the name of a song, artist, or album	"Listen to Everybody Wants to Rule the World"

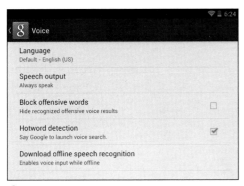

A Voice settings for Google Search.

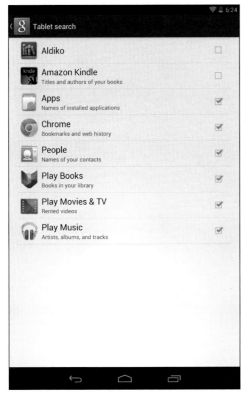

B Tablet Search settings for Google Search.

Setting Search Options

You can control aspects of speech input and output when you search by voice or use voice actions. To view Google Search settings, swipe up from the bottom of the screen to open Google Now (see Chapter 9), scroll to the bottom of the Google Now screen, tap ⋮ > Settings, and then tap any of the following options:

Voice. Voice settings control speech input and output when you search by voice or use voice actions **A**:

- **Language.** Select a language for voice search input and output, which can differ from the language displayed by your Nexus.

- **Speech Output.** Determine whether speech output is on always or on only when a headset is attached to your Nexus.

- **Block Offensive Words.** Determine whether search results with naughty words are blocked.

- **Hotword Detection.** Determine whether you can say "Google" (rather than tap the microphone icon) to initiate voice search or actions from the search bar.

- **Download Offline Speech Recognition.** Install languages for speech recognition when you're not connected to the Internet.

Tablet Search. Select which apps on your tablet are included in Google searches **B**.

Privacy and Accounts. Control the account for use with Google Search and search-related privacy options for that account. The Google Account used with Google Search and Google Now is shown in the Privacy and Accounts screen 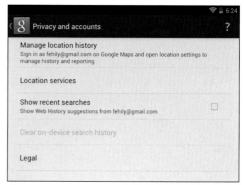.

You can set these options:

- **Manage Location History.** Opens Google Maps settings, where you turn location settings and location reporting on or off.

- **Location Services.** Opens the Settings screen for these services, including Google's location service and GPS. See also "Using Location Services" in Chapter 17.

- **Show Recent Searches.** Determines whether search suggestions are based on your recent searches.

- **Manage Web History.** Opens your Web History settings in a browser, where you can pause or remove your search history. Sign in to your Google Account if necessary. (This option is available only if Show Recent Searches is selected.)

C Privacy and Accounts settings for Google Search.

Maintaining Contacts with People

People, an electronic address book, stores names, addresses, telephone numbers, email addresses, birthdays, anniversaries, and other contact information. Your contacts are available in Gmail, Messenger, Calendar, Navigation, and other apps and services that tap into People.

When you first set up your Nexus and sign into your Google Account, that account's existing contacts are downloaded to your tablet. After that, any changes that you make to your contacts on your Nexus, on the Web, or on another device or smartphone are synced online in the background. Microsoft Exchange contacts can also be synced in this way.

In This Chapter

Using the People App

Open People **A** from the Home or All Apps screen. On the left side, browse contacts by tapping, dragging, or swiping. On the right side, scroll contact info, or tap a field or button to call, email, send a message, video-chat, share a vCard (.vcf) file, show an address in Maps, open a home page, and more.

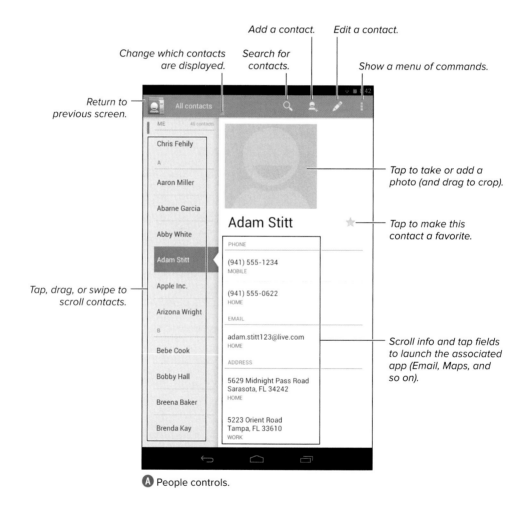

Add a contact.

Edit a contact.

Change which contacts are displayed.

Search for contacts.

Show a menu of commands.

Return to previous screen.

Tap to take or add a photo (and drag to crop).

Tap to make this contact a favorite.

Tap, drag, or swipe to scroll contacts.

Scroll info and tap fields to launch the associated app (Email, Maps, and so on).

A People controls.

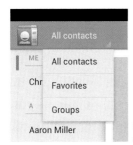

 You can filter certain contacts from view.

Favorite Contacts

You can star contacts to designate them as favorites and then view only starred contacts by tapping Favorites Ⓐ.

To star a contact, tap the contact to view its details and then tap the star ⭐ at the top of the screen to highlight it. You can tap again to unstar a contact and remove it from Favorites view.

Viewing Specific Contacts

By default, People shows all the contacts from all your accounts, but you can view only contacts from one account, from one group, or a custom set of contacts.

To filter contacts:

In the top left corner of the People screen, tap the menu near the 👤 icon Ⓐ.

To change which contacts are displayed:

1. In the top left corner of the People screen, tap the menu near the  icon and then tap All Contacts **Ⓐ**.

2. Tap ⁝ > Contacts to Display.

   The Contacts to Display screen opens **Ⓑ**.

3. Tap All Contacts, tap a specific account, or tap Customize to set up a fine-grained selection.

   If you tap Customize, the Define Custom View screen opens **Ⓒ**. Tap an account to open or close a list of its groups and other categories, and then select those that you want. You can make selections within multiple accounts. When you're done, tap OK.

To change how contacts are displayed:

Tap ⁝ > Settings and then tap a display option **Ⓓ**.

Ⓑ You can specify which contacts from which accounts are displayed.

Ⓒ Categories within accounts can include contacts that you've marked as favorites.

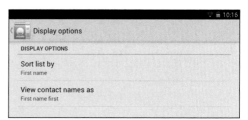

Ⓓ You can sort contacts by first or last name, or display last name or first name initially for each contact (for example, Adam Stitt or Stitt, Adam).

A The Add Contact screen, ready for a new contact.

Adding Contacts

You can add contacts on your Nexus and then sync them with the contacts in your Google Account, your Microsoft Exchange account, or other accounts that support syncing.

To add a new contact:

1. In the top left corner of the People screen, tap the menu near the ● icon and then tap All Contacts.

2. Tap ●+ in the toolbar at the top of the screen.

   The Add Contact screen opens **A**.

3. If you have more than one account with contacts, tap the one to use.

4. Type the contact's name and other information.

   Tap a field to type or choose a value. Swipe up or down to scroll the categories.

5. To add multiple entries for a category, tap Add New for that field.

   You can add a work address after typing a home address, for example.

continues on next page

6. To open a menu with preset labels, such as Mobile or Work for a phone number, tap the label to the right of the item of contact information.

or

To create your own label, tap Custom in the drop-down menu .

7. To add the contact to one or more contacts groups, tap the Groups field.

or

Tap Create New Group in the drop-down menu to add the contact to a new group.

TIP Groups are synced between People on your Nexus and Contacts on the Web. To view or edit contacts on a computer or other device, go to http://google.com/contacts and then sign in.

8. To add other types of contact information, tap Add Another Field 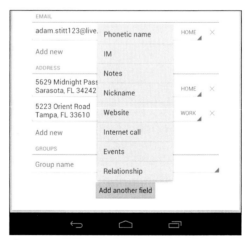.

9. When you're finished, tap Done at the top of the screen 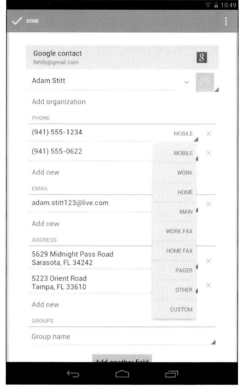.

B The Add Contact screen, being filled out.

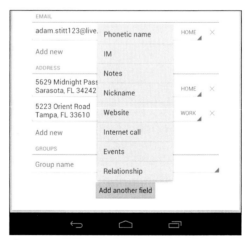

C You can add a variety of contact information. To keep track of birthdays or anniversaries, for example, tap Events in the Add Another Field menu.

Importing and Exporting Contacts

If you copy contacts stored in vCard (.vcf) format to your Nexus, you can import them into People. You can also export all your contacts in vCard format to internal storage and later copy them to a computer or other device.

You need to import your contacts only once. Contacts for your Google Account stay in sync across your Nexus, the Web, and your computers and devices (including new devices that you sign in to).

To import contacts to your Google Account:

On a computer, import your email and contacts from another email account into your Gmail account. In a browser, sign in to your Gmail account at http://gmail.com, click the gear icon ✿ in the top-right corner of your inbox, and then choose Settings > Accounts and Import tab > Import Mail and Contacts link.

or

On a computer, export your contacts from Microsoft Outlook, Mac OS X Contacts, or other address-book or mail app as a file, and then import them into your Google Account via a browser on your computer. The most common file formats used for export/import are CSV (.csv) and vCard (.vcf). In a browser, go to http://google.com/contacts, sign in to your Gmail account, and then choose More > Import.

or

On a computer, export your contacts to a vCard (.vcf) file and then import that file directly on your Nexus, as described in the following section.

TIP To view or edit your contacts on the Web, go to http://google.com/contacts and then sign in.

To import contacts to your Nexus's internal storage:

1. Connect your Nexus to your computer via USB cable.

2. Copy one or more contacts in vCard (.vcf) format to your Nexus's internal storage.

   For details, see Chapter 7.

3. In People on your Nexus, tap ⋮ > Import/Export.

   The Import/Export Contacts screen opens **Ⓐ**.

4. Tap Import from Storage.

5. If you have more than one account on your Nexus, tap the target account.

6. If you have more than one vCard file in storage, choose whether to import a single file, multiple files, or all files **Ⓑ**.

   A message appears on your Nexus until all the contacts are imported. If you don't see them in People, make sure that they're not filtered from view; see "Viewing Specific Contacts" earlier in this chapter.

To export contacts to your Nexus's internal storage:

1. In People on your Nexus, tap ⋮ > Import/ Export.

   The Import/Export Contacts screen opens **Ⓐ**.

2. Tap Export to Storage.

3. Tap OK.

   People creates a vCard (.vcf) file containing all your contacts in your Nexus's internal storage. You can connect your Nexus to your computer via USB cable (see Chapter 7) and then copy this file for use with any application that can work with vCard files, such as email and address-book programs.

Ⓐ The Import/Export Contacts screen.

Ⓑ The Choose vCard File screen lets you choose which contacts to import.

Share contact via

Bluetooth   Dropbox   Email

Gmail   Skype

A The available sharing methods depend on the apps you've installed.

Sharing Contacts

You can share contacts in vCard (.vcf) format by using Gmail, Bluetooth, or other apps and services.

To share a contact from People:

1. In People, tap the contact that you want to share.

2. Tap ⦙ > Share.

   The Share Contact Via screen opens **A**.

3. Tap a method for sharing the vCard: Gmail, Bluetooth, and so on.

4. Use the app that you chose to finish sharing the .vcf file.

   If you choose Gmail or Email, for example, the contact is shared as an email attachment.

Editing Contacts

The screen for editing a contact is the same as the screen for adding a contact.

To edit a contact:

1. In People, tap the contact that you want to edit.

2. Tap 🖊 in the toolbar at the top of the screen.

3. Edit the contact information.

   For editing details, see "Adding Contacts" earlier in this chapter.

4. When you're finished, tap Done at the top of the screen.

Multiply Sourced Contacts

If you edit a contact that contains information from multiple sources, changes made to info from one source don't affect the info from other sources. Instead, the info from each source is grouped in its own labeled section in the contact details.

If you have information about the same contact from a Google Account and a Microsoft Exchange account, for example, and both accounts are configured to sync contacts, edits to the information from the Google Account are synced to that account on the Web, whereas the contact's info in the Exchange account remains unchanged.

See also "Joining or Separating Contacts" later in this chapter.

Read-Only Accounts

If you try to delete a contact from a read-only account such as a Skype or Twitter account, People only *hides* that contact and displays a message to that effect. To restore any hidden contacts, you must delete the pertinent account from your Nexus and then add it again (see Chapter 6).

If the contact contains information from an editable account *and* from a read-only account, a message tells you that the information from the read-only account will be hidden, not deleted.

Deleting Contacts

If you delete a contact from a Google Account (or any account with editable contacts), the contact is also deleted from Contacts on the Web (http://google.com/contacts) when you next sync your Nexus.

To delete a contact:

1. In People, tap the contact that you want to delete.

2. Tap ⋮ > Delete.

3. Tap OK to confirm the deletion.

Joining or Separating Contacts

When you add a new account, People automatically tries to merge duplicate contacts into a single entry. If People guesses wrong, you can join or separate contacts manually. After you do, however, automatic merging no longer works for that contact.

To join contacts:

1. In People, tap the contact that you want to join with one or more other contacts.

   This contact is the one that you'll see in People after the join.

2. Tap 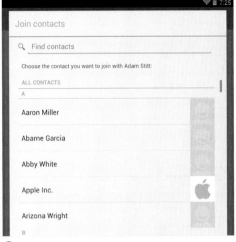 in the toolbar at the top of the screen.

3. Tap ⋮ > Join.

   The Join Contacts screen opens Ⓐ.

4. Tap the contact whose information you want to join with the first contact.

   The information from the second contact is added to the first contact, and the second contact disappears from the People list.

5. Tap Done at the top of the screen.

6. To join another contact to the main contact, repeat the preceding steps.

> **TIP** The Web-based version of Google Contacts also offers a tool to eliminate duplicate contacts. Go to http://google.com/contacts, sign in to your account, and then choose **More > Find & Merge Duplicates.**

Ⓐ You can scroll to a contact or search for contacts by typing in the Find Contacts field.

To separate contacts:

1. In People, tap the contact that you want to separate.

2. Tap 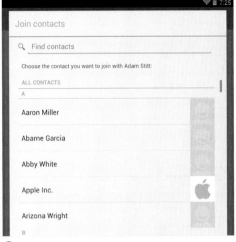 in the toolbar at the top of the screen.

3. Tap ⋮ > Separate.

   The Separate command is available only if the contact information comes from at least two sources.

4. Tap OK to confirm the separation.

   The contact information is separated into individual contacts.

12

Scheduling Appointments with Calendar

Calendar keeps you on schedule and lets you track your life's important events. You can view individual calendars or a single combined calendar, which makes it easy to manage work and personal appointments at the same time.

Using Calendar

Open Calendar Ⓐ from the Home or All Apps screen. Calendar displays events from each of your accounts that synchronizes its calendars with your Nexus. Each account can have multiple calendars available for display, based on the way you've set up that account's calendars in a browser. For Google Accounts, you can set up calendars at http://google.com/calendar.

TIP Agenda view lists your events in chronological order, omitting days without events. A black line indicates where today begins.

Add new event.

Jump to today's date.

Show a menu of commands.

Choose a view.

Return to previous screen.

Drag, pinch, or spread to change the view; tap to add a new event; or swipe to change the date.

Tap to view or edit event.

Tap to show or hide calendars.

Drag or tap to change date.

Ⓐ Calendar controls.

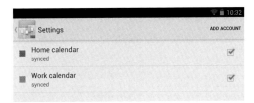

A Events from each calendar are displayed in that calendar's color.

Setting Up Accounts

The Accounts screen (covered in Chapter 6) lets you view or change which of your accounts are synced with Calendar. To sync a Google Account calendar, for example, tap Settings > Google (below Accounts), tap the account whose calendar you want to sync, and then select Calendar.

When you first set up Calendar for a Google Account or Microsoft Exchange account, all the calendars that are displayed when you view that account's calendar in a browser are also displayed in Calendar. You can change which calendars are shown **A**.

Syncing and Viewing Calendars

Calendar offers various settings that let you determine how calendars are synchronized and displayed. In Day or Week view, you can hide the controls at the bottom of the screen for an uncluttered view.

To show or hide an account's calendars:

- In Calendar, tap ⁝ > Settings and then tap the account **A**.

TIP Hiding a calendar doesn't stop it from syncing.

To sync all your calendars manually:

- In Calendar, tap ⁝ > Refresh.

TIP Refresh (as well as automatic sync) requires an Internet connection.

To show or hide controls:

- In Day or Week view in Calendar, tap ⁝ > Show Controls or Hide Controls.

Adding, Editing, and Searching Events

You can add, update, delete, and search for events on any of your calendars, and set Calendar to alert you to upcoming events. If you're traveling, you can make Calendar display event dates and times in a specific time zone.

TIP For Google Accounts, events that you add create or edit in the Calendar app appear both on your Nexus and in Google Calendar on the Web (http://google.com/calendar).

To add an event:

1. Tap 🗐₊ in the toolbar at the top of the screen.

   or

   In Day or Week view, touch and hold a spot at the desired date and time, and then tap New Event.

   The New Event screen opens **Ⓐ**.

2. Enter details about the event, such as the calendar, event name, location, time, and reminders.

3. To invite people, enter their email addresses in the Guests field.

4. When you're finished, tap Done.

   The event is added to the specified calendar, and guests you've added receive an email invitation.

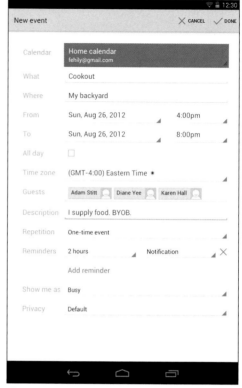

Ⓐ The New Event screen.

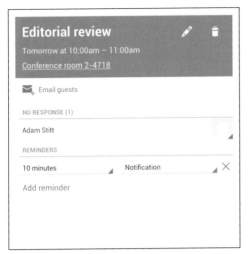

B Tap an event to view its summary, edit it, or delete it.

To edit an event:

1. Tap the event that you want to edit and then tap ✏️ **B**.

   The Edit Event screen opens; it's the same as the New Event screen **A**.

2. Make your changes to the event.

3. When you're finished, tap Done.

   The changes are saved, and updates are sent to any attendees.

To delete an event:

1. Tap the event that you want to edit and then tap 🗑️ **B**.

2. Tap OK to confirm the deletion.

To search for events:

1. Tap ⋮ > Search.

2. Type search terms, or tap 🔍 to speak them.

   Calendar lists matching events for the calendars that you're currently viewing.

To show event times in a specific time zone:

1. In Calendar, tap ⋮ > Settings > General Settings.

   The General Settings screen opens.

2. Select Use Home Time Zone.

3. Tap Home Time Zone and then select a time zone.

Responding to Invitations

If you have a Google, Microsoft Exchange, iCloud, or CalDAV account (such as Yahoo Calendar), you can send and receive invitations.

To invite others to an event, tap Guests while you're adding or editing an event and then type an email address or a name to select invitees from People.

If you receive an invitation, it lands in the scheduled slot on your calendar with a border around the event. To respond, tap the event. You can accept or decline, view the event organizer's contact info, see or email other invitees, or set reminders 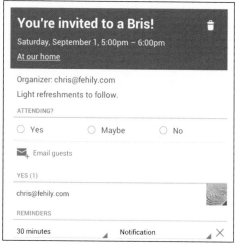.

> **TIP** You can also respond by dragging the notification shade down from the top of the screen and then tapping the event's notification.

Ⓐ Tap an invitation in your calendar to respond to it.

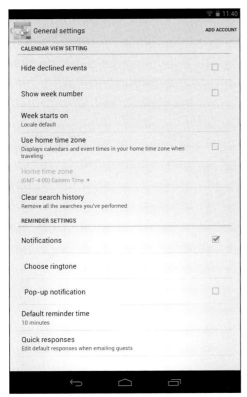

A The General Settings screen for Calendar.

Changing Calendar Settings

To change the settings in Calendar, tap ⦙ > Settings > General Settings and then change any of the following settings **A**:

- **Hide Declined Events.** Determines whether declined invitations appear on your calendars.

- **Show Week Number.** Determines whether the week number appears in Week view.

- **Week Starts On.** Lets you choose the first day of the week: Saturday, Sunday, Monday, or the locale default.

- **Use Home Time Zone.** Determines whether Calendar displays event dates and times using a specific time zone when you're traveling.

- **Home Time Zone.** Lets you choose a specific time zone. This option is available only when Use Home Time Zone is selected.

- **Clear Search History.** Clears your search history in Calendar.

- **Notifications.** Determines whether you receive event notifications. (For details on notifications, see Chapter 8.)

- **Choose Ringtone.** Sets a ringtone (alert sound) for event notifications.

- **Pop-Up Notification.** Determines whether event notifications appear on the main screen.

- **Default Reminder Time.** Sets the lead time for event notifications.

- **Quick Responses.** Allows you to edit default responses that you can use to respond to invitations quickly.

13

Browsing the Web with Chrome

Chrome is the Nexus's Web browser. You can use it to download files and to display Web pages with text, graphics, animations, sounds, video, and links—but not Adobe Flash, Microsoft Silverlight, and Java media, which aren't supported by Android.

Note that the Web is a *portion* of the Internet. (The terms are not synonyms.) The Internet contains not only the Web, but also channels for email, instant messages, and more.

In This Chapter

Using Chrome

Open Chrome from the Home or All Apps screen. The important part of Chrome isn't the app itself, but the access it gives you to Web pages and other online resources. You'll spend most of your browsing time working within the Web itself—reading, searching, scrolling, zooming, tapping links, filling out forms, downloading files, and so on—rather than using Chrome's controls **A**.

TIP Google also releases Chrome for Windows, OS X, Linux, and iOS (http://google.com/chrome).

Bookmark page.

Type a Web address (URL) or search the Web.

Tap a tab to see its page.

Speak search terms.

Navigate recently viewed pages.

Open a new tab.

Show a menu of commands.

Reload or stop page.

Double-tap, pinch, or spread text or graphics to zoom.

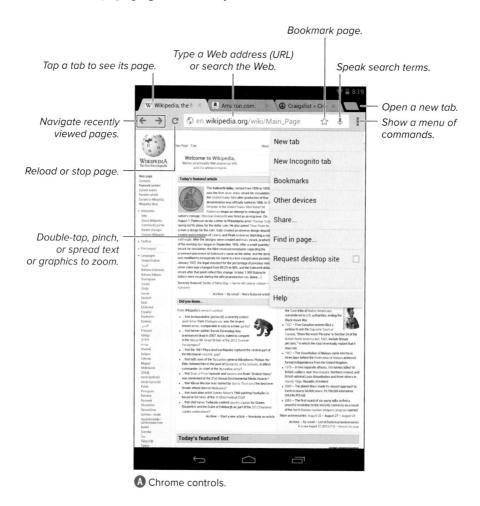

A Chrome controls.

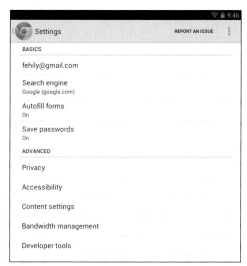

Settings   REPORT AN ISSUE

BASICS

fehily@gmail.com

Search engine
Google (google.com)

Autofill forms
On

Save passwords
On

ADVANCED

Privacy

Accessibility

Content settings

Bandwidth management

Developer tools

A The Settings screen in Chrome. If you're signed in to Chrome, your account's email address appears in the Basics section.

Signing In to Chrome

When you sign in to Chrome with your Google Account, you can take advantage of several Google services, including syncing of bookmarks, search history, and open tabs.

Signing out of Chrome stops syncing but doesn't delete existing data stored on your Nexus and in your Google Account. All future changes within Chrome, however, won't be synced to your account.

To sign in to or out of Chrome:

1. In Chrome, tap ┋ > Settings to open the Settings screen **A**.

2. To sign in, tap Sign In to Chrome in the top-right corner and then sign in.

   If you're already signed in, your email address appears near the top of the screen (below Basics) **A**.

   TIP If you previously encrypted your data, you must enter your password to sign in.

   or

   To sign out, tap your email address near the top of the screen and then tap Disconnect Google Account in the top-right corner.

To set up Chrome services:

1. Tap ⋮ > Settings **A**.
2. Tap your email address (below Basics).
3. Set up the following services **B**:

   ▸ **Sync.** Lets you access your Chrome bookmarks, browsing history, and open tabs from other devices where you're also signed in **C**. To protect your data by using your Google Account password or a custom pass-phrase, tap Encryption. To remove synced data from your account (or reset a forgotten sync passphrase), tap Reset Sync. To enable or disable syncing, use the On/Off slider at the top of the screen.

TIP To take full advantage of sync options, sign in to Chrome on your computer, tablet, or smartphone.

   ▸ **Chrome to Mobile.** Determines whether you can send Web pages from your computer to your Nexus for offline reading on your tablet. On Chrome on your computer, you must install the Chrome to Mobile exten-sion from the Chrome Web Store and then click the Chrome to Mobile icon 🖥 in the address bar.

   ▸ **Auto Sign-In.** Determines whether you must type your account name and password when you use Google services.

B Chrome services.

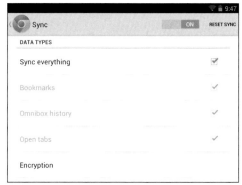

C Sync options in Chrome.

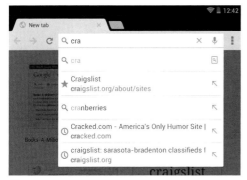

A You can use the omnibox to search the Web or open a specific Web page.

Searching the Web

The *omnibox* (address bar) at the top of Chrome lets you search the Web or visit a specific Web page.

To open a Web page or search the Web:

1. Tap the omnibox at the top of the screen.

2. Type the address of a Web page (URL) or terms to search for **A**.

   As you type, a list of suggestions appears. Icons in the list identify the type of match:

   ▸ The Search icon 🔍 appears next to searches.

   ▸ The Bookmark icon ★ appears next to sites you've bookmarked.

   ▸ The History icon 🕐 appears next to sites from your browsing history.

   ▸ The Globe icon 🌐 appears next to related sites.

   TIP To copy a suggestion to the omnibox, tap the arrow ↖ to its right. Then you can keep typing or choose further suggestions.

3. To search for the contents of the omnibox or open a specific Web address that it contains, tap the Go key on the keyboard.

   or

   To search for a suggestion or go to a suggested Web page, tap it.

   Chrome opens either the specified Web page or a list of search results.

   TIP To change the default search provider, tap ⋮ > **Settings** > **Search Engine**. To toggle suggestions for related queries and popular Web sites, tap ⋮ > **Settings** > **Privacy** > **Search and URL Suggestions**.

Here are a few typing tips:

- Press and hold the .com key to get your choice of .net, .org, .edu, and other top-level domains, depending on what country or region you've set your Nexus for.

- To erase the omnibox quickly, tap × in the right side of the box.

- To speak instead of type, tap 🎤 in the omnibox or the onscreen keyboard. For details, see "Dictating Text" in Chapter 4.

- For general typing tips, see Chapter 4.

URLs

A *URL* (Uniform Resource Locator) is a case-insensitive address that identifies a Web page uniquely. The URL for Google's home page, for example, is http://www.google.com. The transmission standard for most Web pages is http://, so you don't type it; Chrome fills it in for you. Secure (banking and commerce) Web sites use https://. The rest of the address specifies the Web server and the Web page's location on it. Some URLs don't need the www. part; others require additional dot-separated elements.

The server name's last part, called the *top-level domain* (TLD), usually tells you about the Web site's owner or country. The domain .com is a business, .gov is a government, .edu is a school, .uk is a United Kingdom site, .ca is a Canadian site, and so on. For a list of TLDs, see www.iana.org/domains.

Web-page files are organized in folder trees on the server, so a long URL (www.google.com/chrome/features/, for example) works like a path on a computer. Complicated URLs that contain ?, =, and & symbols are pages created on the fly in response to a query, such a product search on Amazon.com.

If a 404 or Not Found message appears instead of a Web page, you may have mistyped the URL, or the Web page may have been moved or removed. (Some Internet providers redirect 404 errors to a page full of sleazy ads.)

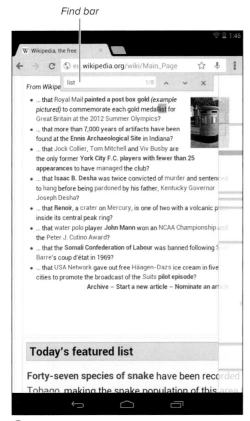

Find bar

A The find bar appears near the top of the screen, below the omnibox.

TIP You can also find text on a page by tapping the boxed magnifying glass 🔍 to the right of an omnibox suggestion.

Navigating Web Pages

You can do any of the following things when you navigate Web pages:

- **Scroll and zoom.** To scroll, swipe or drag in any direction. To zoom in or out, double-tap, spread, or pinch. Web sites that are optimized for mobile devices typically open to a size appropriate for the device and may not permit zooming and scrolling. In some cases, you may prefer to view the desktop (nonmobile) version of a site. Most mobile-optimized sites provide a link (often near the top or bottom of the page) that lets you switch to the big-screen version.

TIP To make text bigger or smaller (without zooming), tap ⋮ > Settings > Accessibility > Text Scaling. You can also force-enable Web-site zooming in Accessibility.

- **Rotate your Nexus.** You can view pages in either portrait (tall) or landscape (wide) view. Web pages scale automatically to the wider screen, making the text and images larger. For details, see "Changing Screen Orientation" in Chapter 2.

- **Revisit pages.** To revisit pages that you've seen recently, tap ← (Back) or → (Forward).

- **Search within a page.** To find text in the current Web page, tap ⋮ > Find in Page **A**. As you type in the find bar, matches are highlighted on the page, and a scroll bar on the right edge shows the relative positions of the matches. The find bar shows the total number of matches. To jump to a match, tap the up and down arrows in the find bar, or tap or drag the scroll bar.

continues on next page

- **Share a page.** To share the address of the current Web page, tap ⁝ > Share **B**.

- **Reload a page.** To reload a stale or incomplete page, tap ↻ in the toolbar.

- **Stop downloading a page.** If you request the wrong page or tire of waiting for a slow-loading page, tap ✕ in the toolbar to stop the page from downloading any further.

- **Follow a link.** Text links typically are colored phrases. Pictures and buttons can also be links. To follow a link, tap it. If you touch and hold a link, you can see where it leads; open it in a normal or incognito tab; copy its URL to the clipboard to paste elsewhere; or download a file **C**.

B The list of available sharing services depends on which apps you've installed.

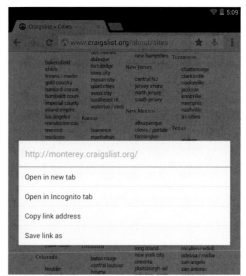

C Touch and hold a link to see where it leads or to open, copy, or download it.

A The Most Visited section on a new tab. To switch sections, tap the name of a section at the bottom of the tab.

Working with Tabs

Like all modern browsers, Chrome features tabbed browsing, which lets you open multiple Web pages on the same screen. You can open pages or links in new tabs and switch among them by tapping tabs.

To view and manage tabs, do any of the following:

- To view a different tab, tap it.

- To open a new tab, tap ▨ or tap ⋮ > New Tab **A**.

  The following sections appear on new tabs to help you find the page you want:

  Most Visited. Shows snapshots of Web pages you've visited recently or repeatedly. Tap a snapshot to visit the site.

  Bookmarks. Lists sites you've bookmarked. Tap an icon to visit the site.

  Other Devices. Lists Chrome tabs that are opened on other devices. Tap a page icon to open the same tab on your Nexus. To use this feature, you must be signed in to Chrome to sync your open tabs across devices (see "Signing In to Chrome" earlier in this chapter).

- To scroll through the list of tabs, swipe or drag tabs left or right.

- To reorder tabs, touch and hold a tab until the other tabs dim, and then drag left or right. Alternatively, touch and hold a tab, and then drag down to the left or right.

continues on next page

- To close a tab, tap × on the tab.

- To reopen a recently closed tab, open a new tab, tap Most Visited at the bottom of the new tab, and then tap a link below Recently Closed 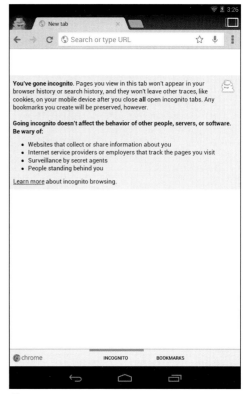.

- To browse in private mode with incognito tabs, tap ⋮ > New Incognito Tab. A new tab opens with an incognito icon and information about going incognito **B**. To switch in and out of incognito mode, tap ☐ in the top-right corner.

  When you're browsing incognito, your browsing history, cookies, and cache are automatically cleared after you close all your incognito tabs. You can still access your normal bookmarks and omnibox suggestions. Changes that you make to bookmarks are saved.

B You can use incognito tabs to browse the Web with more privacy than in normal tabs.

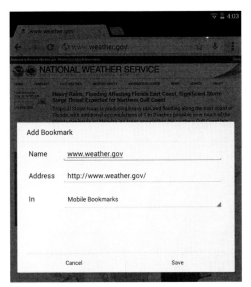

A The Add Bookmark screen.

B The Bookmarks section of a new tab.

Bookmarking Web Pages

You can bookmark Web pages that you like and open them quickly in the future. As your bookmarks list grows, you can organize your bookmarks in folders.

To bookmark the current page:

1. Tap ☆ in the omnibox.

   The Add Bookmark screen opens **A**.

   TIP If a page is already bookmarked, the bookmark icon is solid ★ rather than hollow ☆.

2. If you like, edit the bookmark's name and address.

3. Choose a folder for the bookmark.

   To create a new folder, tap the In menu and then tap New Folder.

4. Tap Save.

To open a bookmarked page:

1. Tap ⋮ > Bookmarks.

   or

   Open a new tab and then tap Bookmarks at the bottom of the tab **B**.

   TIP You can navigate bookmark folders by tapping folder icons or by tapping a folder name just above the bookmark icons (below the omnibox).

continues on next page

2. Tap the bookmark you want.

or

Touch and hold a bookmark icon, and then tap Open in New Tab or Open in Incognito Tab .

To edit or delete a bookmark page:

1. Tap ⋮ > Bookmarks.

or

Open a new tab and then tap Bookmarks at the bottom of the tab **B**.

2. Touch and hold the target bookmark icon, and then tap Edit Bookmark or Delete Bookmark **C**.

TIP You can also tap **Add to Home Screen C** to place a shortcut to a frequently visited Web page on your Home screen.

C Touch and hold a bookmark icon for a menu of commands.

Tap Save Link As to start downloading the file (top). To download a picture, tap Save Image (bottom).

Downloading Files

You can download files via Chrome, Gmail, and other sources onto your Nexus and then manage them by using the Downloads app.

TIP Movies, music, and other media downloaded via the Google Play store don't show up in Downloads.

To download and manage files:

1. Touch and hold the link to the file, and then tap Save Link As (or Save Image) in the dialog box that opens **A**.

    The download proceeds in the background. To track its progress, drag the notification shade down from the top of the screen **B**.

continues on next page

B The notification shade shows the progress of each download to completion.

2. When the download completes, open the Downloads app **C** from the Home or All Apps screen and then do any of the following:

- ▸ To open a downloaded file, tap it, tap an associated app in the Complete Action Using screen that opens, and then tap Always (to always use the selected app to open this type of file) or Just Once (to use this app only this time) **D**.

TIP To control file-type associations, use the **Launch by Default** setting in an app's App Info screen. For details, see "Managing Apps and Services" in Chapter 2.

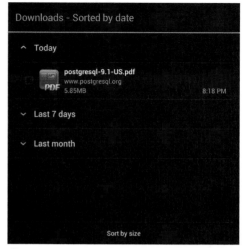

C The Downloads app lists files downloaded via Chrome, Gmail, and other apps.

D The list of available apps depends on which apps you've installed.

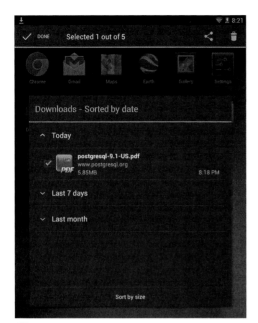

 Tap the check box next to a file's icon to select or deselect the file. When one or more files are selected, a toolbar appears at the top of the screen.

 The list of available sharing services depends on which apps you've installed.

▸ To view earlier downloads, tap one of the date headings (Yesterday, Last 7 Days, and so on) **C**.

▸ To sort files, tap Sort by Date or Sort by Size at the bottom of the screen **C**.

▸ To delete files, select the target files and then tap 🗑 **E**.

▸ To share files, select the target files and then tap ⌁ **F**.

TIP Files available in the Downloads app can also be viewed in the Download folder that's visible when you connect your Nexus to a computer. You can view and copy files from this folder. For details, see Chapter 7.

Changing Chrome Settings

To change the settings in Chrome, tap ⋮ > Settings and then change any of the following settings 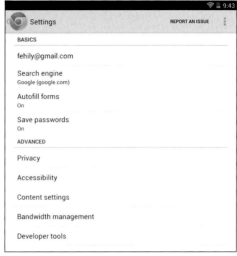:

- **Search Engine.** Choose the default search engine for the omnibox (see "Searching the Web" earlier in this chapter).

- **Autofill Forms.** This feature fills in your name, address, credit-card numbers, and other personal info on Web forms, saving you from typing the same information repeatedly. (Autofill is especially useful for frequent online shoppers.) When you start filling out a form, the autofill entries that match what you're typing appear in a menu. Tap an entry to automatically complete the form with information from the entry.

- **Save Passwords.** This feature memorizes and fills in user names and passwords on Web forms—convenient, but a potential disaster if you ever lose a Nexus that isn't screen-locked. (For details, see "Setting the Screen Lock" in Chapter 3.)

Ⓐ The Settings screen for Chrome.

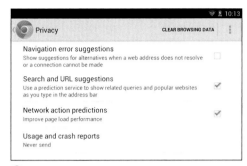

B The Privacy screen for Chrome.

Cookies

Cookies are messages given to Chrome by Web sites and stored on your Nexus as small files. A cookie's main purpose is to identify you and possibly prepare customized Web pages for you. When you enter shopping preferences and personal information at, say, Amazon.com, that information is stored in a cookie, which Amazon can read when you return.

Most cookies are innocuous and spare you from having to fill out forms repeatedly, but some sites and advertisers use tracking cookies to record your browsing history.

■ **Privacy.** This option lets you control personal information (such as Web pages visited) that's sent to Google when you search or browse the Web **B**.

The most useful option is Search and URL Suggestions. When this option is turned on, Chrome uses a prediction service to show you related queries, matches from your browsing history, and popular Web sites as you type in the omnibox (address bar), provided that your default search engine is Google or uses Google's prediction service. Chrome sends the text you type to Google to retrieve suggested searches and sites, which are then displayed in the omnibox menu. Google anonymizes any sent text within a day.

TIP To clear your browsing history, cookies, saved passwords, and other personal data, tap Clear Browsing Data in the top-right corner of the Privacy screen.

■ **Accessibility.** This option makes Chrome easier to use and text easier to read.

■ **Content Settings.** This setting controls the type of content—including cookies—that Web sites can show and the information they can use.

■ **Bandwidth Management.** Chrome's Preload Webpages feature tries to open Web pages faster by predicting which page you're headed to next. Chrome preloads the page's data in the background so that it can open immediately if you tap its link. Preloading can use a large amount of storage, but you can turn it off.

■ **Developer Tools.** This option offers advanced settings for software developers and Web-site authors.

14

Watching YouTube Videos

 Though you can use Chrome (or any browser) to watch YouTube videos at www.youtube.com, Nexus comes with a dedicated YouTube app that makes finding, watching, and keeping track of videos easier.

In This Chapter

Using the YouTube App

Open the YouTube app from the Home or All Apps screen. You can browse and watch videos without a YouTube account, but you must sign in if you want to comment on videos, add them to your playlists, upload videos, and use other personal features. To do so, tap Sign In or tap ⋮ > Sign In on the YouTube Home screen ⓐ.

The Home screen differs depending on whether you're signed in. After you sign in, the navigation bar on the left side of the screen shows your account info and subscription list. The From YouTube section lists content by category. To return to the Home screen at any time, tap the YouTube icon in the top-left corner of the screen (repeatedly, if necessary).

You can swipe the panel to the right of the navigation bar to view it full-screen. To return to the navigation bar, tap YouTube's icon or swipe the panel to the right.

Tap your YouTube username in the navigation bar to view your history, uploads, favorites, playlists, and more.

To change your YouTube account settings, tap ⋮ > Settings. You can resize the caption font, set upload options, clear your search history, and more.

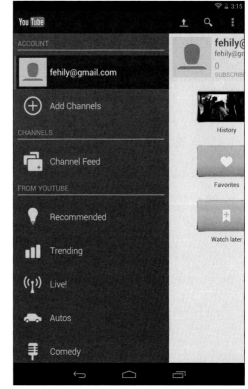

ⓐ The YouTube Home screen.

A A video's Info screen shows a title, number of views, upload date, contributor, viewer ratings, description, and more. Swipe left or right to see links to related videos and viewer comments.

Finding and Watching Videos

Millions of YouTube videos are available, submitted by people around the world. You can watch them in full-screen view or with the video's Info page showing. The playback controls work about the same way that they do in most video apps.

To find and watch a YouTube video:

1. To browse for videos, tap a category in the navigation bar (on the left side of the YouTube Home screen).

   Swipe up or down to scroll the list of categories, if necessary.

   or

   To search for videos, tap 🔍 at the top of the screen and then type search terms. To speak instead of type, tap 🎤 in the search field.

   (For details, see "Dictating Text" in Chapter 4.)

   TIP A YouTube *channel* is a collection of a person's videos, playlists, and other YouTube information. You can open other people's channels and subscribe to them: Tap Add Channels on the Home screen.

2. Tap a video thumbnail or title to see that video's Info screen **A**.

continues on next page

3. If the video doesn't start playing automatically, tap ▶ to play it. To watch full-
screen, rotate the Nexus to landscape
(wide) view.

After a few seconds, the playback controls disappear so that they don't block
the picture. Tap the video at any time to
show or hide the controls **B**.

TIP **If a CC control appears for a video, you
can tap it to toggle closed captions.**

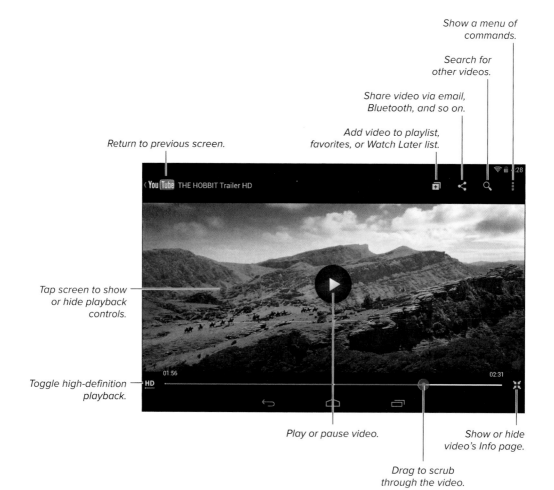

Show a menu of
commands.

Search for
other videos.

Share video via email,
Bluetooth, and so on.

Add video to playlist,
favorites, or Watch Later list.

Return to previous screen.

Tap screen to show
or hide playback
controls.

Toggle high-definition
playback.

Play or pause video.

Show or hide
video's Info page.

Drag to scrub
through the video.

B YouTube playback controls for a full-screen video.

15

Gmail and Keeping in Touch

 Gmail is the Nexus's email app for Google Accounts. Your messages are stored on Google servers, but you can read, write, and organize messages with Gmail on your Nexus or from any Web browser. When you set up your Nexus with a Gmail account, the Gmail app is ready to go.

If you haven't set up an account yet, or if you want to set up another account, tap Settings on the Home or All Apps screen and then tap Add Account. Chapter 6 has the details.

In This Chapter

About Gmail

You can open Gmail from the Home or All Apps screen. Your most recent conversations are displayed in your Inbox. When you return to Gmail after using other apps, the last screen you were working with appears.

Because Google stores your mail on its servers, you can search your entire message history at any time. The servers also sync your actions across devices. If you read a message in Gmail on your Nexus, for example, it's marked as read at http://gmail.com in a Web browser.

Each Gmail message and all its replies are grouped in your Inbox as a single *conversation* that's easy to follow. Traditional email apps, by contrast, spread an original message and its replies across your Inbox, typically sorted by date received and separated by other messages.

You can tag Gmail conversations with multiple standard or custom *labels* to organize them in different ways. In traditional email apps, each message lives in only one folder.

Touring Your Inbox

The first time you open Gmail, it shows a scrolling list of your most recent conversations, placing the one with the most recent messages at the top **Ⓐ**.

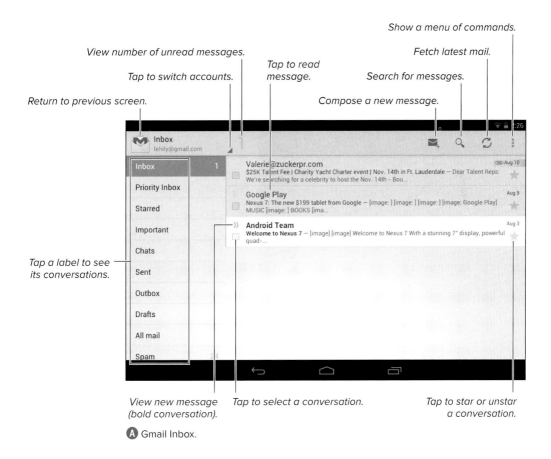

Show a menu of commands.

View number of unread messages.

Fetch latest mail.

Tap to switch accounts.

Tap to read message.

Search for messages.

Return to previous screen.

Compose a new message.

Tap a label to see its conversations.

View new message (bold conversation).

Tap to select a conversation.

Tap to star or unstar a conversation.

Ⓐ Gmail Inbox.

All your conversations are shown in your Inbox unless you delete, archive, or filter them. You can also tap Priority Inbox or any other label in the list on the left side of the screen. Conversations with new messages have bold Subject lines. Small icons tell you about the message:

- » means the message was sent directly to you, and ⟩ means you were copied.

- If you mark a conversation message as important (tap ⋮ > Mark Important), or if you're using Priority Inbox, messages are flagged with » or ⟩.

- If a message was sent to you as part of a group, it has no icon or is marked with ⟩.

By tapping items on the left side of the screen, you can view all conversations that you've starred or that have the same label. To control how labeled conversations are synced, tap ⋮ > Manage Labels and then tap the desired label.

If you're offline, you can read messages synced to your Nexus. You can also compose and send messages, which are stored on your Nexus with the Outbox label until you're back online, when they're sent automatically. By default, Gmail is synced to 30 days.

TIP When you tap 🔍 to find messages, you can search by using terms that appear in message contents, addresses, subjects, labels, and so on.

Priority Inbox

If you get a lot of mail, you may want to use Priority Inbox to separate the wheat from the chaff. If you configure Gmail on the Web (at http://gmail.com) to show Priority Inbox, Gmail on your Nexus will show it as well.

Gmail labels a message important and sticks it in Priority Inbox based on your past treatment of similar messages, how directly the message is addressed to you (To or Cc), and other factors.

To add or remove Priority Inbox conversations manually, you can mark them as important or not important. In any conversation list, tap to select the check boxes of the target conversations and then tap ⋮ > Mark Important or Mark Not Important. Over time, Gmail learns what kinds of messages are important to you.

To set Priority Inbox as your default inbox, tap ⋮ > Settings, tap your account, and then select Priority Inbox.

Reading Mail

Gmail pushes new messages to your Nexus automatically as they arrive. (You don't need to tap anything to retrieve them.) When you get a new message, a notification icon appears in the status bar at the top of the screen. You can drag down from the top of the screen to show the notification shade and a brief summary of the message. (For details, see Chapter 8.)

> **TIP** To toggle notifications for Gmail messages, tap ⋮ > Settings, tap your account, and then tap Email Notifications.

To read a conversation's messages, tap the conversation **A**. A conversation opens to the first new (unread) message or to the first starred message. To reread messages in a multiple-message conversation, tap Previously Read Messages just above the blue bar and then tap one of the earlier messages to expand it.

View sender's name and address.

View sender info or add sender as contact.

Show or hide message images.

Archive conversation.

Delete conversation.

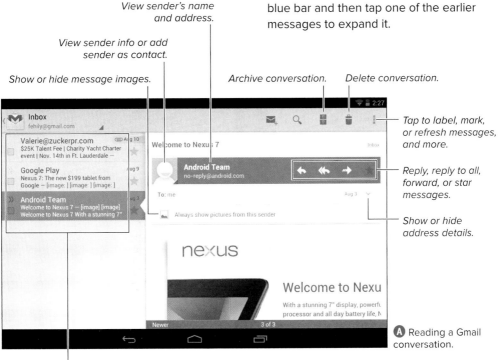

Tap to label, mark, or refresh messages, and more.

Reply, reply to all, forward, or star messages.

Show or hide address details.

A Reading a Gmail conversation.

Tap to read messages.

To move to the previous or next conversation, swipe the message left or right. For details on copying and pasting message text, see "Selecting and Editing Text" in Chapter 4.

TIP A green dot below the sender's name indicates that the sender is available to chat via **Google Talk**.

Archive, Delete, and Mute

Archiving a conversation moves it out of your Inbox without deleting it. Archived conversations are included in search results and are available under the All Mail label and any other labels you've assigned to them. If someone replies to a message that you've archived, its conversation reappears in your Inbox.

When you *delete* a conversation, it's moved under the Trash label, where it's deleted automatically after about 30 days.

If an ongoing conversation wearies you, you can *mute* it to remove it from your Inbox. In your Inbox, select the check boxes of the conversations you want to mute and then tap ⋮ > Mute, or when you're reading a message, tap ⋮ > Mute.

New messages addressed to the group members of a muted conversation bypass your Inbox and are archived automatically. (New messages with your address in the To or Cc field still appear in your Inbox.) To view muted conversations, tap the All Mail label.

A Attachment information in a message.

Working with Attachments

When a message has an attached file, a paper-clip icon ⊂⊃ appears near the sender's name in the message list, and information about the attachment appears at the top of the message **A**.

Depending on the type of attachment, your installed apps, and your settings, Gmail may display a thumbnail image and one or more of the following buttons:

View or Play. Download the attachment (if it hasn't already been downloaded) and then view or play it by using a related app.

Preview. Partially download the attachment and view it in a separate window. For multiple-page documents, Preview downloads only the first few pages to view, which is faster and less space-consuming than View, which downloads the entire attachment.

Info. Show information about the attachment, if no installed app can open it.

TIP You can download apps that open different kinds of files from the Google Play store (see Chapter 16).

Save. Download the attachment and save it on your Nexus.

Downloaded files are available from the Downloads app (see "Downloading Files" in Chapter 13) or in the Download folder when you attach your Nexus to your computer (see Chapter 7).

TIP To download attachments automatically, tap ⫶ > Settings, tap your account, and then tap **Download Attachments**.

Managing Conversations in Bulk

You can archive, label, delete, and perform other actions on multiple conversations at the same time, in your Inbox or another conversation list. In a conversation list, select the check boxes of the conversations that you want to work with as a group and then choose an action **A**.

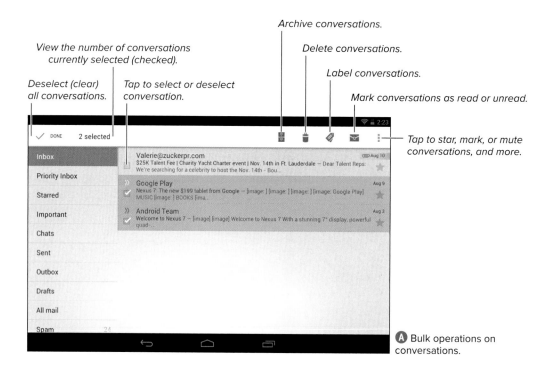

Archive conversations.

View the number of conversations currently selected (checked).

Delete conversations.

Label conversations.

Deselect (clear) all conversations.

Tap to select or deselect conversation.

Mark conversations as read or unread.

Tap to star, mark, or mute conversations, and more.

A Bulk operations on conversations.

A Replying to a message.

Replying and Forwarding

If you reply to a message, files or photos attached to the original message aren't sent back. To include attachments, forward instead of reply.

In replies and forwards, you can tap Respond Inline to interleave your message with the text of the old one.

In replies, you can turn off Quote Text to exclude the message you're replying to from the text of the new message (also removing any attachments or formatting in the original message).

Replying to or forwarding messages without changing the subject adds your reply to the current conversation. Changing the subject starts a new conversation.

All the messages in the conversation, up to the one you're replying to or forwarding, are included in the new message; any messages that follow the message you're responding to are omitted.

Writing and Sending Mail

You can use Gmail to write (compose) a message and send it to anyone who has an email address.

To write and send a message:

1. View a list of conversations or a message.

2. To start from scratch, tap ✉+ at the top of the screen.

   or

   To continue a conversation by replying to or forwarding one of its messages, tap Reply ↰, Reply All ↰, or Forward ⇢ in the blue message header.

   Whatever you do, Gmail creates a new message A.

3. If you have multiple Gmail accounts, tap the From field at the top of the message and then choose the account to send from.

4. To add a recipient, tap the To field and then type the recipient's email address.

   If the recipient is a contact in your People list, Gmail autosuggests addresses as you type (which you can tap or ignore).

TIP To remove a recipient, tap it and then tap the × that appears next to it.

continues on next page

5. If you want to send copies of the message to other people, tap +CC/BCC to the right of the To field; then tap the Cc (carbon copy) or Bcc (blind carbon copy) field, and fill it out as you did the To field.

> **TIP** Bcc recipients aren't disclosed to the message's other recipients. It's common to use Bcc when you're addressing many recipients or recipients who don't necessarily know one another (members of a mailing list, for example).

6. Tap the Subject field and then type whatever this message is about.

If you're replying to or forwarding a message, you can edit the existing subject (which starts a new conversation).

7. To attach a photo or file, tap the paper-clip icon ⊜ to the right of the Subject field.

> **TIP** To remove an attachment, tap × to the right of the attachment's name.

8. Tap the Compose Email area and then type your main text.

> **TIP** For tips on typing on the onscreen keyboard, see Chapter 4.

9. When you're done, tap ➤ Send in the top-right corner of the message, or tap ⋮ to discard the message or save it as a draft for later.

> **TIP** If you're not online, sent messages are stored with the Outbox label until you're online again.

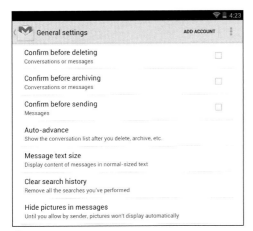

General settings ADD ACCOUNT

Confirm before deleting
Conversations or messages

Confirm before archiving
Conversations or messages

Confirm before sending
Messages

Auto-advance
Show the conversation list after you delete, archive, etc.

Message text size
Display content of messages in normal-sized text

Clear search history
Remove all the searches you've performed

Hide pictures in messages
Until you allow by sender, pictures won't display automatically

Ⓐ The General Settings screen for Gmail.

Changing Gmail Settings

You can change general or account-specific settings in Gmail.

To change general settings, tap ⋮ > Settings > General Settings and then change any of the following settings Ⓐ:

- **Confirm Before Deleting.** Determines whether you must confirm that you want to delete a message.

- **Confirm Before Archiving.** Determines whether you must confirm that you want to archive a message.

- **Confirm Before Sending.** Determines whether you must confirm that you want to send a message.

- **Auto-Advance.** Lets you choose which screen opens when you delete or archive a conversation whose messages you're viewing.

- **Message Text Size.** Makes message text larger or smaller for more comfortable reading.

- **Clear Search History.** Removes all terms you've searched for in Gmail.

- **Hide Pictures in Messages.** Restores the default pictures setting (doesn't show pictures automatically) for all senders.

To change account-specific settings, tap ⋮ > Settings, tap the account name, and then change any of the following settings **B**:

- **Priority Inbox.** Determines whether Priority Inbox is your default inbox, so it (instead of Inbox) opens when you start Gmail and have new messages. You receive notifications only for new messages that are part of important conversations (rather than for every new message). This setting is available only if you've configured Gmail on the Web (at http://gmail.com) to show Priority Inbox.

- **Email Notifications.** Determines whether you receive a notification when you get a new message. For details, see Chapter 8.

- **Ringtone & Vibrate.** Fine-tunes notifications and ringtones (alert sounds) for notifications on a per-label basis. This setting is available only if Email Notifications is turned on.

- **Signature.** Adds an optional personalized tag to the bottom of each outgoing message. Typically, a signature is your name, title, contact info, or—if you must— a favorite quote or legal disclaimer.

- **Gmail Sync is ON/OFF.** Indicates whether Gmail syncing is turned on or off for this account in the main Settings app.

- **Days of Mail to Sync.** Sets the number of days' worth of email that you want to sync automatically.

- **Manage Labels.** Manages which conversations are synced.

- **Download Attachments.** Determines whether message attachments are downloaded when you receive them, rather than requiring you to download them explicitly.

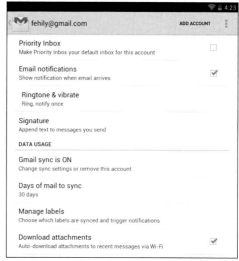

B The Account settings screen for Gmail.

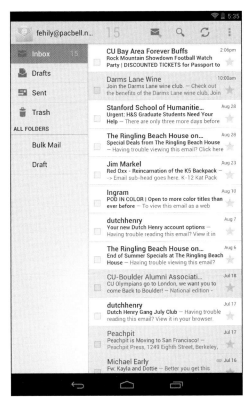

Using Other Apps for Keeping in Touch

The Nexus comes with a few other apps for email, texting, and video chat.

Email. You can use the Email app to read and send email from services other than Gmail, such as Yahoo, Hotmail, AOL, iCloud, and Microsoft Exchange. To set up an account, tap Settings on the Home or All Apps screen and then tap Add Account. Chapter 6 has the details.

The Email app **A** isn't too different from the Gmail app, the main differences being that Email doesn't support conversations or labels. Instead, each message is listed separately and stored in only one folder. If you're using multiple email accounts, you can view all messages in all accounts by using Combined view. (Tap the account name near the top of the screen and then tap Combined View.)

A The Email app.

POP and IMAP Mail

When you set up a non-Gmail account (by tapping Settings > Add Account), use the account settings provided by your Internet service provider (ISP), account administrator, or employer. These settings include your email address, your password, and the addresses of your provider's incoming and outgoing mail servers (which look like *mail.servername.com* and *smtp.servername.com,* respectively).

POP (Post Office Protocol) accounts use an older messaging protocol that wasn't designed to check mail from multiple computers. Unless your provider saves copies of your mail on its server, a POP server transfers incoming mail to your computer (or Nexus) before you read it. You won't get copies of messages when you log in from another computer because you've already downloaded them.

IMAP (Internet Message Access Protocol) servers keep all your mail online, letting you get the same mail on any computer or device you use. IMAP servers track which messages you've read and sent. If you run out of mailbox space on the IMAP server, you must delete old messages to prevent any new incoming mail from bouncing back to the senders. Most popular Web-based providers (Gmail, Yahoo, and so on) and modern organizations use IMAP.

Talk. Google Talk lets you chat with your friends by text, voice, or video. It's the same as the Chat feature in web-based Gmail (at http://gmail.com). Icons in Google Talk, Gmail, Google Maps, and other apps indicate your and your friends' Google Talk status. You can change your online status, the status message displayed beside your name for others, and the picture that others see. Your Google Talk Friends list contains friends that you've invited or accepted invitations from through Google Talk. Friends can see other friends' online status and block messages from one another.

TIP **For video chat, the popular Skype app is available in the Google Play store (see Chapter 16).**

 Messenger. Google Messenger complements Google Talk and lets you send messages to your Google+ contacts. Messenger works only if you're signed up with Google+, a social network that's basically Google's version of Facebook. (For details, go to http://plus.google.com.) Messenger shows a list of all people in your circles, with those you've chatted with recently listed at the top.

Shopping for Apps and Media

 Google Play is Google's digital app and media distribution service. It includes an online store for music, movies, TV shows, books, magazines, and Android apps and games. You can access Google Play on the Web at https://play.google.com/store or use the Play Store app on your Nexus. Your purchases are available across your computers and Android devices. Your Nexus comes with dedicated apps for playing music, watching video, and reading books and magazines that you get from the Google Play store.

In This Chapter

Accessing the Google Play Store

To access the Google Play store, open the Play Store app from the Home or All Apps screen **A**.

TIP To change settings for Play Store, tap ⁝ > Settings.

Unintentional Purchases

As you browse the Google Play store, you may accidentally tap—and buy— something you don't want. To set a personal identification number (PIN) code to prevent unintentional purchases, tap ⁝ > Settings > Set or Change PIN. To reset a forgotten PIN, on the Home or All Apps screen, tap Settings > Apps, scroll to and tap Google Play Store, and then tap Clear Data.

Note that your Google Play PIN isn't the same as—and is less secure than— a screen-lock PIN or password. (See "Setting the Screen Lock" in Chapter 3.)

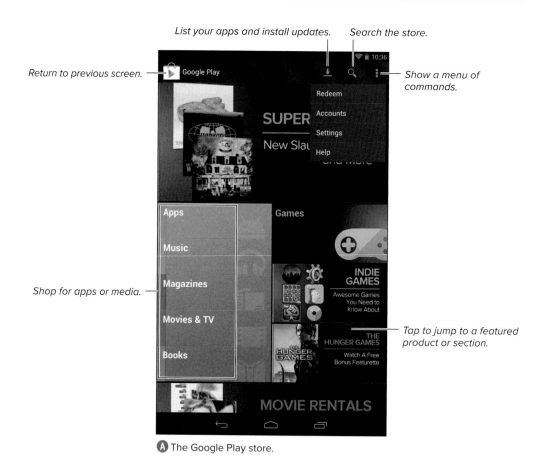

List your apps and install updates.

Search the store.

Return to previous screen.

Show a menu of commands.

Shop for apps or media.

Tap to jump to a featured product or section.

A The Google Play store.

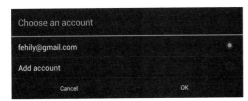

B Your Google Play downloads and purchases are linked to your Google Account.

C The Google Wallet app, the first time you open it.

To shop in the store, you must have a Google Account. To choose an existing account or create a new one, tap ⋮ > Accounts **B**. To manage your accounts, see Chapter 6.

You have several ways to pay for store purchases:

- **Google Wallet.** You can connect your Google Account with Google Wallet to pay for purchases from Google Play (and other online stores). Google Wallet is a secure mobile payment system (similar to PayPal) that lets you store debit cards, credit cards, loyalty cards, gift cards, and more. To set up or sign in to Google Wallet, open the Wallet app on your Nexus **C**, or go to https://www.google.com/wallet.

- **Gift cards.** Google Play gift cards are available in various cash denominations. To find a retailer, go to https://play.google.com/about/giftcards. To redeem a gift card, tap ⋮ > Redeem in the Play Store app, or go to https://play.google.com/redeem. Redeemed cards appear in your Google Account as part of your Google Play balance.

TIP At this writing, Google Play gift cards are available only in the United States and can be used only for content sold in U.S. dollars.

- **Store credits.** In some cases, Google awards free Google Play credit to people who buy Google products or sign up for Google Wallet or other services. Credits appear in your Google Account as part of your Google Play balance.

Getting Apps and Games

To get apps or games from the Google Play store, open the Play Store app from the Home or All Apps screen, tap Apps, and then do any of the following:

- **Browse for apps.** Swipe left or right to browse by category or see featured, top, or trending apps 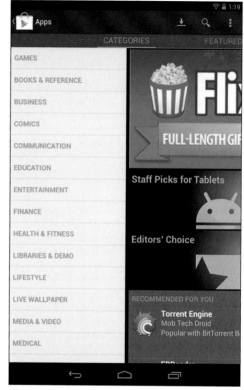.

- **Search for apps.** Tap 🔍 at the top of the screen and then type keywords such as the name of the app or developer. Initially, your history of recent searches appears. As you type, Google Play autosuggests terms **B**. To find free apps, include the word *free* in your search. Tap a suggestion or tap the 🔍 key to see a list of matching apps. To speak instead of type, tap 🎤 in the search field or on the onscreen keyboard. (For details, see "Dictating Text" in Chapter 4.)

TIP To clear your search history, tap ⋮ > **Settings > Clear Search History.**

Ⓐ The Apps screen of the Google Play store.

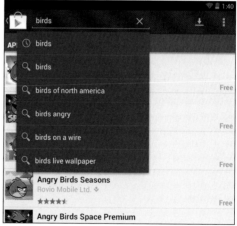

Ⓑ Searching for apps.

C The Details screen for an app.

D The notification shade shows download progress for apps.

- **Install an app.** Browse to or search for the app that you want. Tap the app's icon to see its Details screen **C**, where you can read a description, see screen shots, read customer ratings and reviews, and more. To install the app, tap the app's price (or tap Install). In the dialog box that opens, tap Accept & Buy (or Accept & Download) to accept the permissions for the app (or tap off the dialog box if you don't want to download). The app starts downloading immediately and lands on your Home and All Apps screens.

TIP If you've already downloaded the app, Uninstall and Open appear instead of a price or Install. If an update is available for an installed app, Update appears.

Most apps download in less than a minute, but you can check progress on the app's Details screen or by dragging the notification shade **D** down from the top of the screen. (For details, see Chapter 8.)

- **Share an app.** To send a link to an app's Play Store page via email or another sharing app, tap ⟨ at the top of the app's Details screen **C**.

continues on next page

- **Return an app for a refund.** You have 15 minutes from the time of download to return a purchased app for a full refund. To return an app, tap ⬇ at the top of the screen, tap the app you want to return, and then tap Refund. If you paid by using a debit card, refunds may take a few days. If Uninstall appears instead of Refund, the 15-minute deadline has passed; to get a refund, try contacting the developer directly. (Contact info is in the Developer section of the app's Details screen Ⓒ.)

> **TIP** You can return a given app only once. If you buy the same app again, you can't return it a second time.

- **Uninstall an app.** To remove an app from your Nexus, tap ⬇ at the top of the screen, tap the app to uninstall, and then tap Uninstall Ⓔ. Uninstalling an app also deletes the data, settings, and documents associated with that app.

> **TIP** To uninstall an app quickly without opening Play Store, tap ⊞ in the Favorites tray on the Home screen, touch and hold the icon of the target app, and then drag it to the word *Uninstall* at the top of the screen.

- **Update apps.** Developers occasionally update their apps with bug fixes, new features, and other improvements, and then release the new version through the store. If any updates are available, a notification icon appears in the status bar at the top of the screen. You can drag the notification shade down from the top of the screen to see how many updates are available Ⓕ.

    To update apps, tap ⬇ at the top of the screen. Available updates are listed in the My Apps screen Ⓖ. To update all your apps, tap the Update button near the top-right corner of the

Ⓔ Tap Uninstall to remove an app from your Nexus.

Ⓕ The notification shade tells you whether app updates are available.

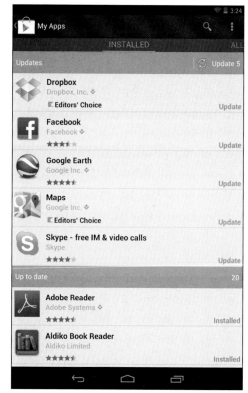

Ⓖ The My Apps screen.

screen. To update any single app (or learn more about an update), tap the app to show its Details screen **C** and then tap Update **H**. If you want this app to autoupdate in the future, select the Allow Automatic Updating check box. To make *all* apps autoupdate, tap ⁝ > Settings > Auto-Update Apps.

TIP To change notification settings for app updates, tap ⁝ > Settings > Notifications.

TIP To manage installed apps, see "Managing Apps and Services" and "Optimizing Data Usage" in Chapter 2.

H The Details screen for an app with an update available.

Can't Find an App?

If you can't find an app, try different search terms, in case the app's name has changed. Also, an app won't appear if it doesn't run on your Nexus because the developer targeted it for a different screen size, Android version, country, or whatever. It's also possible that a publisher removed the app from the store.

The store is curated, meaning that Google can yank an app from the store if it crashes too much, violates store policy, is complained about excessively, or whatever. Yanked apps disappear from the store but not from your Nexus; after you download an app and back it up, it's yours.

Playing Music

 To get music from the Google Play store, open the Play Store app from the Home or All Apps screen and then tap Music. The store's Music screen opens Ⓐ. Swipe left or right to browse by genre or to see featured or top songs and albums. Or tap 🔍 at the top of the screen to search for music. Availability varies by country. When you find what you want, tap to sample or buy it.

To listen to your music, use the Play Music app Ⓑ, which you can open from the Home or All Apps screen; alternatively, tap the headphones icon at the top of the Music screen Ⓐ. Music purchases from Google Play appear in the app automatically, and you can add more songs from your personal music collection on your computer. Play Music can do the things common to most digital music players: create playlists, queue songs, adjust equalization, manage your music library, share songs, stream online music, and so on.

TIP **To manage your music collection on your computer, go to https://play.google.com/music and install the Google Play Music Manager.**

Ⓐ The Music screen of the Google Play store.

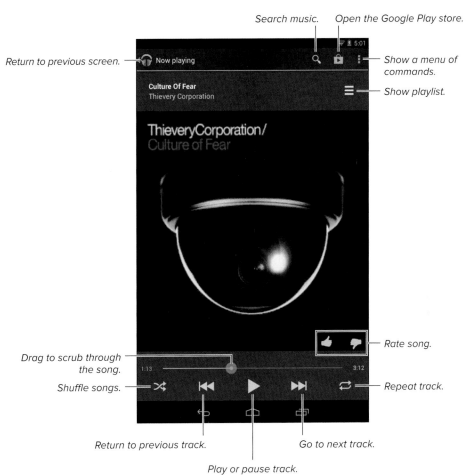

Search music.

Open the Google Play store.

Return to previous screen.

Show a menu of commands.

Show playlist.

Rate song.

Drag to scrub through the song.

Shuffle songs.

Repeat track.

Return to previous track.

Go to next track.

Play or pause track.

B The Now Playing screen in the Play Music app.

Playing Movies and TV Shows

 To get movies and TV episodes from the Google Play store, open the Play Store app from the Home or All Apps screen and then tap Movies & TV. The store's Movies & TV screen opens Ⓐ. Swipe left or right to browse by category or to see featured or top movies and TV shows. Or tap 🔍 at the top of the screen to search for videos. Availability varies by country. When you find what you want, tap to preview, rent, or buy it. Some videos, labeled HD, are in high-definition format.

 To watch movies or TV shows, use the Play Movies & TV app Ⓑ, which you can open from the Home or All Apps screen; alternatively, tap the filmstrip icon at the top of the Movies & TV screen Ⓐ. Movie and TV purchases from Google Play appear in the app automatically, and you can add personal videos that you copy over to your Nexus via a USB cable (see Chapter 7).

> **TIP** Play Movies & TV can play videos in H.263, H.264/AVC, MPEG-4, or VP8 format, but the Google Play store has plenty of third-party media players, such as MX Player, that can play AVI, MKV, and other popular video formats.

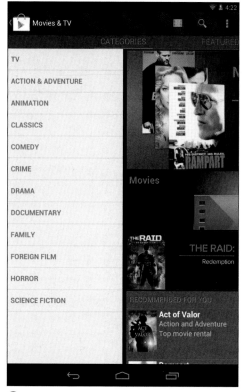

Ⓐ The Movies & TV screen of the Google Play store.

Watching Video on Your HDTV

To watch movies or TV shows from Google Play on your high-definition television (HDTV), you need a Micro-USB–to–HDMI cable. After you connect your Nexus to your HDTV, the Nexus screen should be *mirrored* on your HDTV (both devices display the same content), with the audio playing on your HDTV. Don't forget to change the TV's input source to the correct HDMI connection.

Play or pause video. *Show a menu of commands.*

Return to previous screen. *Toggle widescreen and full-screen display.*

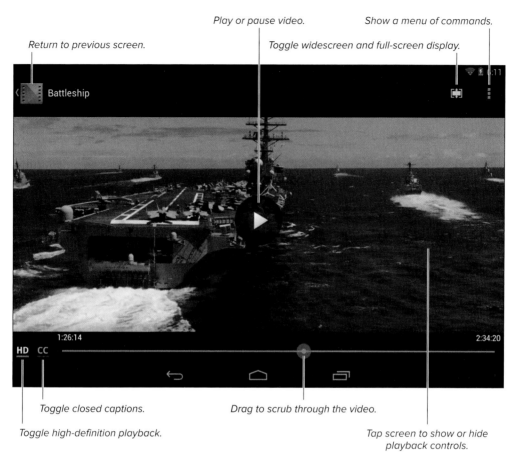

Toggle closed captions. *Drag to scrub through the video.*

Toggle high-definition playback. *Tap screen to show or hide playback controls.*

B Play Movies & TV app.

Reading Books

 To get books from the Google Play store, open the Play Store app from the Home or All Apps screen and then tap Books. The store's Books screen opens **A**. Swipe left or right to browse by category or to see featured, new, or top books. Or tap 🔍 at the top of the screen to search for books. Availability varies by country. When you find what you want, tap to sample or buy it (or download a free book).

To read books, use the Play Books app **B**, which you can open from the Home or All Apps screen; alternatively, tap the book icon at the top of the Books screen **A**. Books purchases from Google Play appear in the app automatically. Play Books supports books in EPUB or PDF format.

TIP You can't add your own books, or books from other bookstores, to your Play Books library. But plenty of readers—such Adobe Reader, Aldiko Book Reader, and FBReader— are available in the Google Play store, as well as bookstore apps like Amazon Kindle and Barnes & Noble Nook.

A The Books screen of the Google Play store.

Search in book.

Show table of contents and bookmarks.

Show book info.

Change font, brightness, and more.

Return to previous screen.

Show a menu of commands.

Swipe or tap page edges to flip pages.

Tap page center to show or hide reading controls.

Return to previous position in book.

Drag or tap to scrub through book.

B Play Books app.

Reading Magazines

 To get magazines from the Google Play store, open the Play Store app from the Home or All Apps screen and then tap Magazines. The store's Magazines screen opens . Swipe left or right to browse by category or to see featured, top, or new magazines. Or tap 🔍 at the top of the screen to search for magazines. Availability varies by country. When you find what you want, tap to subscribe to the magazine or buy an issue.

To read magazines, use the Play Magazines app **B**, which you can open from the Home or All Apps screen; alternatively, tap the magazine icon at the top of the Magazines screen **A**. Magazine purchases from Google Play appear in the app automatically. All magazine subscriptions autorenew when your current term expires. You can cancel your subscription before the end of the subscription term in the Play Magazines app or at https://play.google.com/magazines.

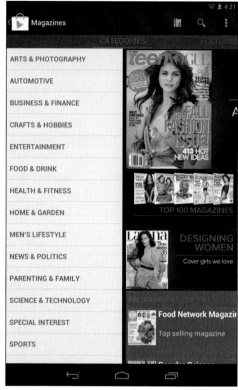

 The Magazines screen of the Google Play store.

Free Trials

When you subscribe to a magazine with a free trial, you get the current issue plus any new issues published within the trial period. All trials last at least 14 days.

You must enter credit-card information, but you won't be charged until after the trial period. If you cancel your subscription during the trial, you won't be charged, but you can still read the issues that you got as part of the trial. You can get one free-trial period per magazine.

Google Currents

Google Currents is a magazine app that aggregates free content from a wide variety of sources that you can choose among. Publishers contribute in-depth articles, videos, photos, slideshows, live maps, and social streams. New stories are available throughout the day. If you use Google Reader (http://google.com/reader), you can turn your favorite blogs and feeds into a custom "magazine." You can open Google Currents from the Home or All Apps screen.

Resize text and strip ads (if available).

Return to previous screen.

Show a menu of commands.

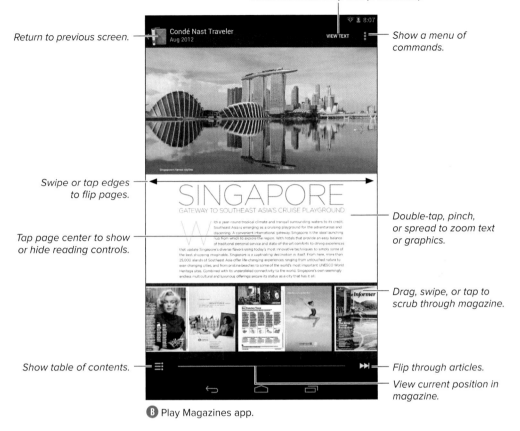

Swipe or tap edges to flip pages.

Tap page center to show or hide reading controls.

Double-tap, pinch, or spread to zoom text or graphics.

Drag, swipe, or tap to scrub through magazine.

Show table of contents.

Flip through articles.

View current position in magazine.

B Play Magazines app.

Finding Your Way with Maps

Google Maps is one of the crown jewels of the Nexus. With it, you can

- See your location on a map
- Move, pan, and zoom the map
- Search for locations
- Get details about businesses and points of interest
- Use a compass
- View street-level images
- Get directions to travel via car, public transit, bicycle, or foot
- See real-time traffic information
- Layer geographic information on maps

Other apps let you view satellite imagery, navigate with voice guidance, see your friends' locations and status messages, and browse local places.

In This Chapter

Using Google Maps

Open the Maps app from the Home or All Apps screen. A map appears, color-coded and labeled with streets, points of interest, borders, parks, bodies of water, geographic features, and much more .

Find and center your current location, or enter Compass mode.

Get directions.

Search for locations.

Show a menu of commands, show features, or clear map.

View your current location.

Use multitouch gestures to navigate the map, or touch and hold to show location info.

A Google Maps.

Here are some housekeeping tips for Maps:

- Unless you're viewing an offline map (see "Saving Offline Maps" later in this chapter), Maps needs a continuous Internet connection to update its cartographic and point-of-interest data, so don't rely on it for emergency directions or wilderness hikes.

- Certain Maps features, such as My Places and Latitude, use your Google Account. If you're not already signed in to your account by tapping Settings > Accounts (see Chapter 6), you can sign in from within Maps: Tap ⋮ > Settings > Sign In. (The Sign In command doesn't appear if you're already signed in.)

- You must turn on Location Services to view your location in Maps, use your location to find nearby places, and report your location to apps that request it. See "Using Location Services" later in this chapter.

Navigating the Map

You can move, zoom, rotate, and tilt the map.

To move the map:

- Drag the map.

To rotate the map:

- Spread your thumb and index finger, and touch them to the map; then rotate them clockwise or counterclockwise.

  or

  Keep your fingers steady and rotate the Nexus itself.

To zoom the map:

- To zoom in, double-tap a map location with one finger—repeatedly, if necessary 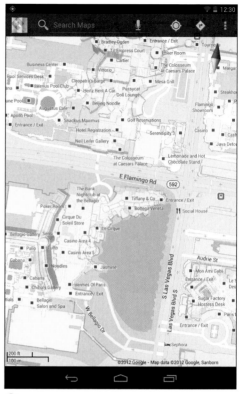.

  or

  To zoom out, tap once with two fingers—repeatedly, if necessary.

  or

  Touch the map with two fingers and then spread them to zoom in or pinch them to zoom out.

TIP The map's scale bar in the bottom-left corner changes as you zoom. To toggle zoom buttons or the scale bar on the map, tap ⁝ > Settings > Display.

A A zoomed-in map can show a surprising amount of detail, including points of interest; one-way-street indicators; businesses; transit stops; and even indoor floor plans for some airports, stations, museums, malls, stores, and hotels.

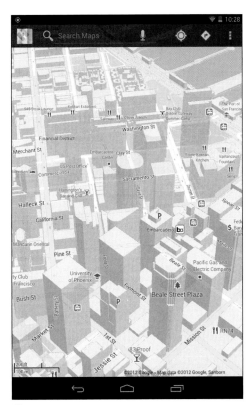

B At lower zoom levels, a tilted (angled) map shows 3D buildings for some cities.

To tilt the map:

- Drag two fingers from top to bottom on the map **B**.

  To return to overhead view, drag two fingers from bottom to top. To return to overhead, north-up view, tap the compass icon at the top of the screen.

Viewing Location Details

You can get the address and other information about an area on the map.

To view location details:

1. Touch and hold a location, star, or labeled feature, or select a search result on the map.

   A small info window opens over the location, displaying the name or address and a thumbnail image or icon **A**.

2. Tap the info window to open a place window with additional details about the location **B**.

   From the place window, you can get directions, explore Street View, see public photos, write or read reviews, and more. The amount of information depends on the location.

TIP Ads may appear in the various windows of Maps.

A An info window for a location.

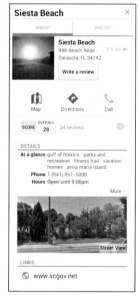

B A place window for a location.

Clearing the Map

If the map becomes cluttered with windows or cartographic details, you can return it to its default view, showing only the base map. Clearing the map is often useful before you search for a location, layer the map, get directions, or navigate.

To clear the map:

- In map view, tap ⋮ > Clear Map.

  Search results, directions, layers, windows, and selected places are cleared from the map, and the map returns to the default view.

Using Compass Mode

Compass mode shows an angled view of the area around you, oriented in the direction in which you're facing or moving.

> **TIP** The Nexus's built-in magnetometer serves as a compass.

To start Compass mode:

1. Tap the My Location icon at the top of the screen.

   The icon turns into a compass rose ◈.

2. Tap ◈.

   The map orients in the direction that you're facing and shifts from overhead view to an angled view **Ⓐ**.

To exit Compass mode:

- Tap ◈ again.

> **TIP** Compass mode is also available in Street View. (See "Exploring Street View" later in this chapter.)

Your current location and direction   *Red tip of compass pointing north*

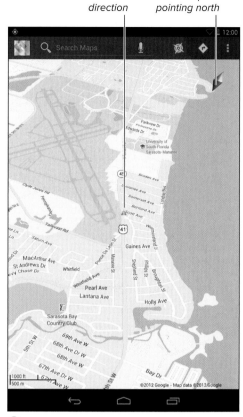

Ⓐ The map in Compass mode.

Your current location and direction

(A) The map in Compass mode.

Finding Your Location

The My Location feature centers the map on your approximate current location by using a variety of methods to determine your location.

TIP For help finding nearby restaurants, attractions, and more, tap ⋮ > Local or (in landscape view) tap the Local icon 🔲 at the top of the screen. To find offers from nearby businesses, tap ⋮ > Offers.

To see your location on the map:

- Tap the My Location icon ◉ at the top of the screen.

  The map centers on a blue arrow that indicates your location (A).

TIP The diameter of the circle around the arrow (visible when you zoom in) indicates the location's precision. For details, see "Using Location Services" later in this chapter.

Exploring Street View

Street View shows ground-level photos merged into a 360-degree panoramic view. Street View isn't available for all locations.

To show Street View:

1. Touch and hold a location on the map to open a small info window above the location.

2. Tap the info window to open the location's place window .

3. In the place window, tap the Street View button (if available).

   Street View opens **Ⓑ**.

4. Do any of the following:

   ▸ To move down a street, double-tap.

   ▸ To pan the view, swipe or drag.

   ▸ To zoom, pinch or spread.

   ▸ To jump quickly to a point, drag the Pegman icon 👤 from the bottom-left corner to that point.

   ▸ To tilt, pan, or turn the Nexus to change the view, tap ⋮ > Compass Mode.

> **TIP** The Nexus's built-in accelerometer and magnetometer sense how you're holding the Nexus in physical space.

   ▸ To exit Street View, tap ⋮ > Go to Map, or tap the Street View icon in the top-left corner.

Ⓐ Street View is available from a location's place window.

Ⓑ Street View.

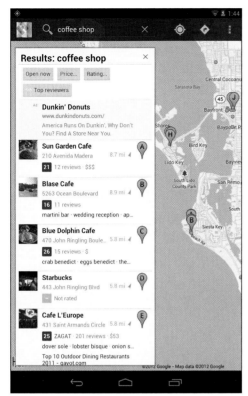

A The Results window lists matching places, and lettered map markers show the corresponding locations.

Searching for a Location

You can search for bodies of water, geographic features, latitude–longitude coordinates, continents, countries, regions, provinces, states, cities, towns, neighborhoods, street addresses, postal or zip codes, roads, intersections, airports (names or three-letter codes), landmarks, parks, schools, businesses, and other points of interest. Partial words and misspellings sometimes work.

To search for a location:

1. If you like, clear the map of existing search results and other details: Tap ⋮ > Clear Map.

2. If you're going to search for a local, nonspecific location, such as *coffee shop* or *movies,* scroll and zoom the map to narrow the area of interest, or tap ◉ to zoom to your current location.

3. Tap the search field at the top of the screen and then type a location.

   Initially, your history of recent searches appears. As you type, Maps autosuggests places.

4. Do one of the following:

   ▸ Tap a suggestion or tap the 🔍 key to see a list of matching places.

   ▸ Tap a result in the list or a marker 📍 on the map **A**.

   TIP To speak instead of type, tap 🎤 in the search field or the onscreen keyboard. For details, see "Dictating Text" in Chapter 4.

continues on next page

- To find a previously starred place, a recently found location, a place on an offline map, or another important location, tap ⋮ > My Places.

- To find nearby restaurants, bars, attractions, and other places, tap ⋮ > Local, or (in landscape view) tap the Local icon 📍 at the top of the screen.

To clear your search history:

On the Home or All Apps screen, tap Settings > Apps, tap Maps in the list of apps, and then tap Clear Data.

Sample Searches

In addition to ordinary street addresses, Maps can find a surprisingly wide range of locations. Experiment. Here are some sample searches:

5th & broadway

1 market st, san fran

honolulu

pizza

asia

mcdonalds beijing

strait of hormuz

mariana trench

mt fuji

half dome

-22.9083, -43.2436 (latitude–longitude)

big ben

disney world

80309 (zip code)

nw1 3hb (postal code)

école polytechnique

greenwich village

lax (airport code)

A base map cleared of layers.

Layering Maps

Layers let you view locations and additional information overlaid on the map. You can toggle individual layers to show or hide traffic, satellite imagery, public-transit lines and stations, Wikipedia info, and more.

To layer the map:

1. If you like, clear the map of existing layers and other details: Tap ⋮ > Clear Map **A**.

2. Tap ⋮ > Layers, or (in landscape view) tap the layers icon ☰ at the top of the screen.

   The Layers window opens, listing layers as well as shortcuts to any recent searches **B**.

> **TIP** The My Maps layer toggles personalized maps that you create at https://www.google.com/maps/mm.

continues on next page

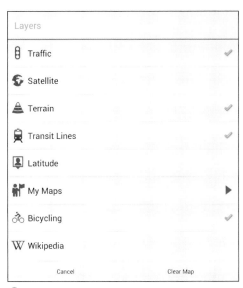

B The Layers window.

3. Tap a layer to toggle it on or off.

If you turn on a layer, it remains on the map until you turn it off or clear the map. Depending on the layer, its information overlays the base map or changes it entirely **C**.

TIP To turn off all layers, you can tap Clear Map at the bottom of the Layers window **B**.

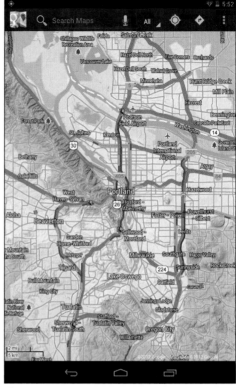

C A map with multiple layers.

The Traffic Layer

Where traffic information is available, the traffic layer shows current, color-coded traffic conditions on highways and roads:

- **Green:** More than 50 miles per hour or 80 kilometers per hour
- **Yellow:** 25–50 mph or 40–80 kph
- **Red:** Less than 25 mph or 40 kph
- **Red/black:** Stop-and-go traffic
- **Gray:** No data available now

These speeds don't apply to traffic on smaller roads and city streets. The colors for roads with low speed limits instead denote traffic severity: green = good, yellow = fair, and red or red/black = bad.

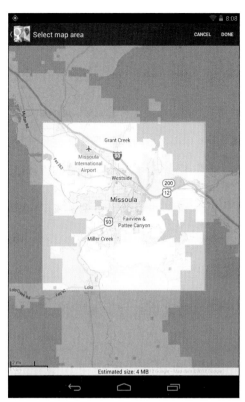

A Position the map area that you want to save within the blue box.

Saving Offline Maps

Offline maps let you select and download certain areas of the map to view even when you're not connected to the Internet. Offline maps are handy when you're traveling outside Wi-Fi coverage.

You can download up to six maps, provided that you have sufficient storage space on your Nexus. Each map itself also has a maximum size, so you may have to split maps of large or dense areas into several smaller saved maps.

Features that need an Internet connection—such as directions and navigation—aren't available offline.

TIP To check your storage space, on the Home or All Apps screen, tap **Settings > Storage.**

To download an offline map:

1. Pan and zoom the map to the area that you want to save, and then tap ⋮ > Make Available Offline.

   or

   Tap ⋮ > My Places > Offline > New Offline Map, and then type a region or city name, or select an area on the map.

2. Pan and zoom the map within the area selector to fine-tune the area to save **A**.

   The estimated size of the selected area appears at the bottom of the screen.

TIP You may see black outlines indicating areas where you've already saved an offline map.

3. When you're finished, tap Done.

To view or manage offline maps:

1. Tap ⋮ > My Places > Offline **B**.

2. Tap a map to open it, or tap ▼ to rename it, delete it, or cancel a map as it downloads.

TIP To delete all your offline maps in one shot, tap ⋮ > Settings > **Offline and Cache** > **Clear All Map Files.**

B Each offline map is listed with its name, save date, and size.

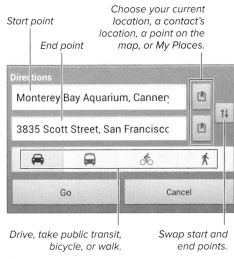

Start point

End point

Choose your current location, a contact's location, a point on the map, or My Places.

Drive, take public transit, bicycle, or walk.

Swap start and end points.

A Directions screen.

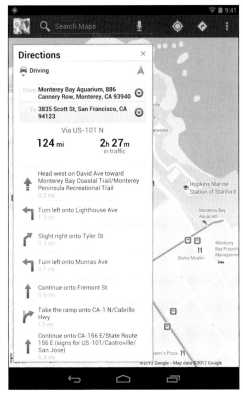

B Directions to your destination.

Getting Directions

Maps can get you from Point A to Point B whether you're driving, walking, bicycling, or taking public transit (bus, train, or ferry). Depending on the route, not every mode of transportation may be available.

To get directions:

1. If you like, clear the map of existing directions and other details: Tap ⋮ > Clear Map.

2. Tap ⬧ at the top of the screen.

   The Directions screen opens **A**.

3. Enter your origin and destination, and tap a transportation method.

   Enter street addresses or search for locations as described in "Searching for a Location" earlier in this chapter.

4. When you're done, tap Go.

   The Directions screen displays the route's step-by-step directions, travel time, and other travel information **B**.

continues on next page

5. Do any of the following:

- ▸ Scroll the list to see all the steps.
- ▸ Tap a step to see that leg of the trip on the map.
- ▸ Tap the origin, destination, or transportation method to change it.
- ▸ Tap ⋮ to reverse the route, update it, or set other route options.
- ▸ Tap ⬘ to launch turn-by-turn GPS navigation. (See "Using Other Mapping Apps and Services" later in this chapter.)

TIP If you chose public transit, you can schedule your trip by using the real-time transit options sourced from public transportation agencies (where available).

6. To see the partial or entire route on the map, tap × to close the Directions window and then pan and zoom the map to show the route 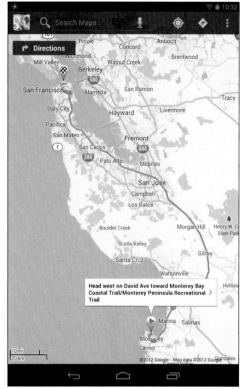.

To reopen the Directions window, tap the Directions button in the top-left corner of the map.

TIP To overlay the current traffic conditions on the route, see "Layering Maps" earlier in this chapter.

Ⓒ Map showing the overall route.

Bike Directions

For some routes, you can get directions for cyclists. These routes are created by using different kinds of roads and paths, color-coded on the route:

- ■ **Dark green:** Bike trail with no motor vehicles
- ■ **Light green:** Street with bike lanes
- ■ **Green/white:** Street recommended for cyclists, but without bike lanes

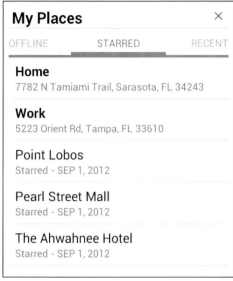

My Places   ✕

OFFLINE   STARRED   RECENT

Home
7782 N Tamiami Trail, Sarasota, FL 34243

Work
5223 Orient Rd, Tampa, FL 33610

Point Lobos
Starred - SEP 1, 2012

Pearl Street Mall
Starred - SEP 1, 2012

The Ahwahnee Hotel
Starred - SEP 1, 2012

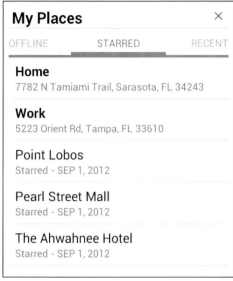 The My Places window.

Using My Places

The My Places window 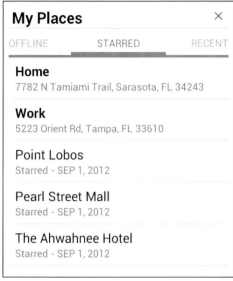 gives you quick access to your important locations and Maps history.

To open My Places, tap ⋮ > My Places. Swipe left or right or tap tabs to see the following:

- Offline maps

- Starred places, including Home and Work locations

TIP To star the current location in Maps, tap ★ in its place window, or tap ⋮ > **Add Star.**

- Recently viewed Maps locations

- My Maps (created at https://www. google.com/maps/mm)

- Checked-in places (in Google Latitude)

- Places that you rated

TIP You can touch and hold an item in My Places for more actions, such as mapping, editing, and deleting.

Using Other Mapping Apps and Services

The Nexus comes with other mapping apps and services that you can launch from the Home or All Apps screen or from inside Maps.

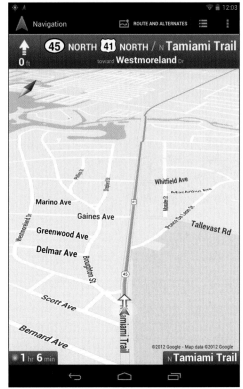

Google Maps Navigation. Navigation Ⓐ offers turn-by-turn GPS navigation with voice guidance, similar to that of handheld GPS navigators like those from Garmin and TomTom. Navigation's features include time to destination, directions listing, traffic conditions, satellite view, Street View, Search Along Route, alternative routes, compass heading, automatic rerouting, volume controls, background navigation, notifications, and voice actions such as "Navigate to..." (see Chapter 10).

To work optimally, Navigation needs a continuous Internet connection, which is possible on the road if you share a cellular Internet connection from your smartphone or personal hotspot with your Nexus. Without an Internet connection, Navigation can still provide voice guidance as long as you don't deviate from your original route, though the underlying map tiles may not update. When you're offline, the navigation icon in the status bar at the top of the screen is gray instead of blue. To stop navigating, tap ⋮ > Exit Navigation.

Ⓐ Google Maps Navigation.

Google Earth. Google Earth **B** features satellite images and aerial photos merged into a virtual globe. You can "fly" to any place around the world and toggle various layers to superimpose place names, businesses, shared photos, Wikipedia articles, 3D buildings, and more. You can pan, zoom, rotate, and tilt the maps. The Earth Gallery offers additional layers—such as country tours, earthquake maps, surfing spots, and hurricane paths—shared by people around the world.

B Google Earth.

Google Local. To get help finding nearby restaurants, attractions, and more, tap ⋮ > Local, or (in landscape view) tap the Local icon at the top of the screen **C**.

Google Offers. To see money-saving offers from nearby businesses, tap ⋮ > Offers **D**.

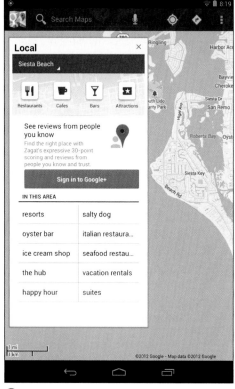

C Google Local.

D Google Offers.

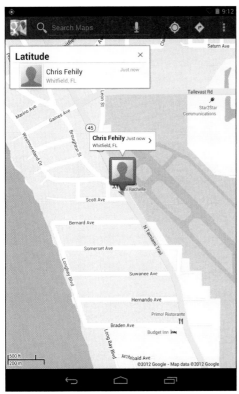

Google Latitude. To share your map location and status updates with friends, and let them share likewise with you, tap ⋮ > Latitude **Ⓔ**. You can also check in at places to let friends know you're there.

To share your location, you must turn on Latitude: Tap ⋮ > Settings > Location Settings. You can turn Latitude off at any time, manage friends, or control how much info you share with friends. You can view and manage your private location history (and see where you're spending time) on the Maps Settings screen or at http://google.com/locationhistory.

Ⓔ Google Latitude.

Using Location Services

Location Services lets apps use your physical whereabouts via the Nexus's built-in positioning service. Built-in apps such as Maps, Chrome, and People use Location Services, as do many third-party apps—particularly weather, travel, search, movie-time, real-estate, and social-networking apps.

Location Services determines your location by combining readings from the Nexus's built-in GPS (Global Positioning System), readings from its digital compass (magnetometer), and data from nearby Wi-Fi hotspots.

Depending on data quality and other factors (such as interference from your surroundings), your location may be unavailable or inaccurate. Apps that show your location onscreen, including Maps, indicate your current location as a blue arrow or dot surrounded by a circle (visible when zoomed in) that indicates how precisely your location can be determined. The smaller the circle, the greater the precision.

If you don't want to be found, or if you want to conserve battery power, you can turn off Location Services. On the Home or All Apps screen, tap Settings > Location Services and then tap the appropriate check boxes Ⓐ.

To determine whether an installed app is using Location Services, tap Settings > Apps, swipe to the All list, and then tap the target app to open its App Info screen. If Your Location is listed below Permissions, the app uses Location Services Ⓑ.

When you download an app from the Google Play store (see Chapter 16), the app's Accept & Buy (or Accept & Download) screen tells you whether the app uses your location.

Ⓐ Location Services screen.

Ⓑ The Permissions section of an App Info screen.

Managing Photos with Gallery

Gallery is the central app for viewing and managing photos that you've taken with your Nexus's camera; copied from your computer; or saved from email, text messages, or the Web. Gallery can display photos and graphics in JPEG, GIF, PNG, BMP, or WEBP format.

You can also use Gallery to view and manage videos that you take with the built-in camera or copy from your computer. Gallery can play videos in H.263, H.264/AVC, MPEG-4, or VP8 format.

In This Chapter

Getting Photos
onto Your Nexus

By default, Gallery displays your photo collections grouped into albums **A**.

TIP To set account and sync options for your pictures, tap ⁞ > Settings.

Tap to show photos in other views.

Return to previous screen.

Show a menu of commands.

Albums show name and number of photos.

A Albums view in Gallery.

You can get photos onto your Nexus in the following ways:

Built-in camera. Photos and videos taken with the Nexus's built-in camera appear automatically in the Camera album in Gallery. The Nexus doesn't come with a built-in camera app, but you can download a third-party app—such as Camera Launcher for Nexus 7 or Instagram—from the Google Play store (see Chapter 16). You can also snap a photo by tapping a contact's image placeholder in the built-in People app (see Chapter 11). The camera's 1.2-megapixel resolution makes for less-than-stunning images, however, and it's awkward taking anything but self-portraits with a front-facing camera.

Downloaded images. To save an attached image from an email message, tap Save in the attachment's info box at the top of the message . (For details, see "Working with Attachments" in Chapter 15.) To save an image from a Web page, touch and hold the image, and then tap Save Image in the dialog box that opens. You can similarly save an image from an instant message. Saved images land in the Download album in Gallery.

B Tap Save to download a photo attached to an email message.

> **TIP** You can manage downloads by using the Downloads app. For details, see "Downloading Files" in Chapter 13.

Copied from computer. Connect your Nexus to your Windows PC or Mac via USB cable and then copy image or video files to your Nexus's internal storage. (For details, see Chapter 7.) You can copy files to anywhere in the Nexus's internal storage and Gallery will find them, but it's more sensible to organize your photo and video collection in the Nexus's Pictures folder. If you copy a folder of photos to your Nexus, that folder becomes an album in Gallery.

> **TIP** You can also transfer files wirelessly via Bluetooth. See "Bluetooth Devices" in Chapter 5.

Screen shots. To capture an image of whatever is on your Nexus's screen (like the figures in this book), press and hold the Power/Lock button and the Volume Down button at the same time for a second. The shot lands in the Screenshot album in Gallery. When you take a screen shot, a notification icon appears in the status bar at the top of the screen. You can jump to the screen shot quickly in Gallery by dragging the notification shade down from the top of the screen and then tapping the screenshot notification.

A Selecting an album reveals controls at the top of the screen.

B Thumbnail images of photos.

Working with Albums and Photos

Here are some tips for working with albums and photos:

- To share, delete, or get details about an album, touch and hold the album to select it, and then use the controls that appear at the top of the screen **A**.

TIP You can also tap ⋮ > **Select Album to select albums.**

- After selecting an album, you can tap others to select multiple albums for bulk operations. Selected albums have a blue border. To deselect a selected album, tap it.

- To see thumbnail images of all the photos in an album, tap the album **B**. Swipe left or right to see all the thumbnails. To see a slideshow, tap ▶. To regroup the album's photos, tap ⋮ > Group By.

TIP Some groupings require time-stamped photos or geotagged photos taken with a GPS-enabled camera.

- In thumbnail view **B**, tap a thumbnail to view the photo full-screen **C**. Rotate your Nexus for the best view. Pinch, spread, or double-tap to zoom the photo. Drag to pan a zoomed photo. Swipe left or right to view other photos in the album. Tap the photo to show or hide controls to share, delete, edit, rotate, and more.

TIP To delete photos quickly, view a photo full-screen **C**, pinch it until you see a series of thumbnails, swipe left or right to the target photo, and then drag it up or down until it fades away.

continues on next page

- In thumbnail view **B**, you can touch and hold a photo to select it and then use the controls that appear at the top of the screen **D**.

> **TIP** You can also tap ⦙ > **Select Item** to select photos.

- After selecting a photo, you can tap others to select multiple photos for bulk operations. Selected photos have a blue border. To deselect a selected photo, tap it.

- Tapping ⦙ > Edit **D** accesses some moderately sophisticated editing tools. You can adjust exposure, apply artistic effects, change colors, crop, fix red-eye, straighten, and more **E**. Tap the buttons at the top of the screen to undo ↺ or redo ↻ your changes. When you edit a photo, a copy is created, and the original is left untouched.

C A full-screen photo, with controls showing.

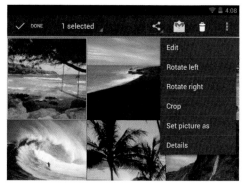

D Selecting a photo reveals controls at the top of the screen.

E A photo with editing tools visible.

Index